KISSES FROM NIMBUS

From SAS to MI6:
An Autobiography

P. J. 'Red' Riley

Clink
Street

London | New York

Published by Clink Street Publishing 2017

Copyright © 2017

First edition.

ISBNs:
978-1-911525-77-6 paperback
978-1-911525-78-3 ebook

TO THE MEMORY OF MY FRIENDS

KAUATA MARAFONO MBE
(FRED)

CAPTAIN WILLIAM G BOOTH
(RICHARD)

SUNDAY 20th JANUARY 1990
14.35 HOURS

A mark, a target, a victim. What do you call a person you are about to kill? I certainly don't want to personalise this whole sordid business by applying a name, but I will at least apply a gender – Male. That's it then – He. He was sleeping peacefully on his back. How odd, I thought. Surely most people sleep lying on one side or the other in the foetal position. It gives them the comfort of still being in the womb I suppose. But lying, quite still, face up, seems to be making it so easy for me – just asking to be suffocated.

I had spent the past twenty-two years of my life in the British Army. The last six of which were in the now famous and very much publicised Special Air Service. Now, after leaving the Army I have been recruited and trained as an agent in Her Majesty's Secret Intelligence Service, otherwise known as MI6 or SIS.

It is well known that, being SAS trained, it is quite easy for me to live for at least a fortnight with nothing more than a pair of old leather bootlaces to suck on for sustenance, and, with steely cold resolve, I can send a heavily armed terrorist to his maker with just a well-aimed swift jab here or there – what a load of bollocks! I know I have to kill this man but I don't know how to. I have no weapon. No trigger to pull, before I close my eyes to avoid the instant when white hot metal smashes into soft body tissue. I have my hands, of course, but they hardly seem adequate and they are shaking.

Throughout my Army career, the closest I ever came to hand to hand combat was as a young soldier in basic training, being taught the finer points of bayonet drill. This consisted of fixing a six-inch steel bayonet to the end of my self-loading rifle, which had to be kept highly polished to avoid the risk of infection. The rifle also had to be kept in pristine condition to avoid I know not what and, charging towards a sack full of straw whilst screaming some ridiculous obscenity, plunge the bayonet hard into the sack. A twist for maximum internal organ damage, keep on screaming, withdraw the bayonet and continue running to the NAAFI truck for sausage baps and tea.

My training as a killer continued but the much-preferred method was with a gun. I spent days, weeks, months even, on rifle ranges across the United Kingdom and Germany. From one hundred metre ranges for pistols and small submachine guns, to the fifteen hundred metre ranges for support weapons, such as the Bren gun or the new, state of the art, general-purpose machine gun. Whatever the weapon the emphasis was always the same – shoot to kill! Shoot to kill has always been an overriding policy of the British Army – there is no other way. Aim for the centre of the target to maximise the possibility of a hit. It matters not where the target is hit, since, in the heat of battle, it can be argued that a wounded soldier could be more of a liability to his comrades than a dead soldier. Whilst the enemy are dealing with their wounded they are less likely to be able to return fire. When it comes to killing, it is generally agreed that it is better to have as much distance as possible between the dispatcher and the recipient. A double tap from a pistol if necessary, but a better option would be a burst of automatic fire from a machine gun at two hundred metres or so. An even better option would be a single shot from a sniper rifle from as far away as a thousand metres, which would surely avoid witnessing the last look of horror as the bullet slams into the victim. Best of all, of course, is to get on the radio and call for air support for fighter ground attack aircraft to carpet bomb the complete area and keep the whole nasty business as impersonal as possible. So yes, I suppose I do qualify as a trained killer, but firing rockets, or bullets at some barely discernible target hundreds of metres away somehow doesn't seem like killing, even if you keep your eyes open and watch the targets fall.

What I am contemplating now is killing a man whose face I can clearly see, a young man, a handsome man, and I have no weapon to make things easier. The bed he is sleeping in is a hospital bed, a small private room with just one bed, two chairs, a small bedside cupboard and a hand wash basin. The single window in the room looks out onto a dirty grey stone wall. I draw the curtains across to prevent any casual, unsuspecting, passer-by witnessing a murder. Even with the curtains drawn there is still enough light in the room to clearly see the man's face.

My recently completed training to become a fully operational SIS agent certainly made no mention of 'How to kill a sleeping man without alerting nearby nursing staff'. What I had been taught included basic 'Tradecraft' (the skill of being as 'grey' as possible and being perceived as anything but a British Secret Agent). My training also included surveillance and anti-surveillance techniques, loading and unloading dead letterboxes to collect and receive messages covertly, photography, practical disguise, communications, defensive driving, and a police advanced driving qualification.

I quietly left the room and walked, a little nervously, towards the toilets and the hospital exit. Although the young female nurse on duty was clearly of Asian descent, she was dressed in a western-style blue and white nurses uniform. She looked up and seemed to eye me suspiciously as I approached the nurse's station.

'Everything okay Mr Riley, is there anything I can help you with?' she said in perfect English with, what I guessed, was a Lancastrian accent.

'No thanks,' I replied, 'He's sleeping like a baby.'

'Can I get you a cup of tea or 'owt?' she asked.

Definitely, I thought, a Lancastrian accent!

'No, we are just fine thanks.' I smiled, 'Be good if he can get a couple of hours' sleep. I'll give you a call if we need anything.'

'Right-o luv,' she said.

On second thoughts she could be from the other side of the Pennines I suppose.

As I washed my hands I stared hard at myself in the mirror. Are you insane, are you *really* capable of doing this? Why not just keep on walking towards the exit and leave the poor bastard in peace?

My handlers in London had made it abundantly clear to me that if, or more likely when, the shit hit the fan, I would be completely on my own. Part of the deal I have signed up for is to be totally deniable to the United Kingdom government. I have been assured that everything possible will be done to help me, but it will be done covertly. Overtly, it will be denied that I have anything whatsoever to do with the British Secret Intelligence Service.

Returning to the room I gave the nurse a friendly smile as I passed, which was acknowledged with nothing more than a nod. Back in the room, he was still fast asleep and thankfully, still on his back. Feeling reasonably confident that we were unlikely to be disturbed, I convinced myself that it had to be now or never. It had to be now. Suffocation seemed to be my only realistic option but there were only two pillows in the room and he was sleeping soundly on both of them. I decide not to risk waking him by trying to get to one of the pillows. On the side of the wash basin, there was a small face cloth which I decided would have to be my weapon. I examined the face cloth. It looked and felt rather porous. I carefully folded the weapon once, then twice. It was still big enough to cover his nose and mouth, but it continued to look somewhat inadequate for what I was about to do. Perhaps soaking the cloth with water would make the material stick together more, I thought, and therefore make the weapon more efficient. I soaked the cloth under the running water. I didn't want it to be too hot or too cold. For some obscure reason, it was important for me to have the weapon at just the right temperature. I approached the bedside knowing what I had to do next. He was resting peacefully, taking short, regular and shallow breaths. Facing directly towards the ceiling, his position seemed to make it almost too easy for me to cover his mouth and nose with the improvised weapon. Getting to within an inch of his face his eyes opened wide, and he frantically grabbed my wrists with both his hands. With unexpected strength, he pushed my hands away and gasped for breath. He had an odd expression of bewilderment on his face as he stared into my eyes. After such a rude awakening, it took a few moments for him to seem to understand what I was trying to do. His expression changed. He assumed, what appeared to me to be a faint smile. He then nodded to me and closed his eyes. I again went about my planned suffocation, but for some reason, I hesitated and stopped short of actually snuffing out the young man's life. His eyes remained closed. He raised his hands, but this time not to push me away, instead he brought his hands together as if in prayer. His body relaxed. His arms fell to his sides. He stopped breathing. Lying motionless his face very quickly turned a deathly grey. As I stood in amazement the weapon dropped from my hand and I realised for certain that he was dead.

Peace at last for my dear brother Howard.

HOWARD

Howard was a beautiful man. He was born profoundly deaf, as were my elder sister Patricia, and my younger brother Craig. My sister Jackie and I were the only two siblings with normal hearing. The deafness in the family was, apparently, caused by some incompatibility between my parents' blood types.

Howard's adolescent years were tough for him as he struggled with his speech difficulties due to his profound loss of hearing. He was often the butt of local youths' jokes and behind his back, he could be teased remorselessly. I regularly got myself into fights in my efforts to protect him, finding it hard to understand their childish cruelty. I became acutely aware of the propensity for young people to ruthlessly take the piss out of Howard and as soon as I noticed the slightest smirk or snide remark, I would round on them with my fists – sometimes without genuine justification. This period of his life got even tougher when he decided to come out and live his life as a gay man.

As an adult, things got much better for Howard and he was no longer the object of petty jokes but became very popular and respected locally. He was intelligent and had a wicked sense of humour. Howard's ability to lip-read was outstanding and he managed to communicate with most people with remarkable ease. He grew confident and was happy to go anywhere on his own despite my mother's insistence that he needed someone to look after him. He soon developed a desire to travel but his local bus trips and train journeys did little to appease his wanderlust and so he got himself a passport and decided that he was going to see the world.

And see the world he did!

I dread to think how many times Howard must have been told that he wouldn't be able to manage travelling to different countries with his inability to speak or hear. But Howard paid not the slightest heed. As soon as he could save enough money for an airline ticket he would be on his way. At first, it was no further afield than Spain. Soon after that, it was America;

California, Florida and Hawaii. He was convinced that there were no limits to where he could, and would, travel. At home in Accrington, he sometimes held down three jobs at once for him to save enough for his next trip to ever more exotic locations.

It was on a trip to Florida with the friends he loved, that he contracted the HIV virus which rapidly developed into full blown AIDS.

At that time the public's perception of HIV/AIDS, Human Immunodeficiency Virus and Acquired Deficiency Syndrome, almost amounted to mass hysteria. Government leaflets were distributed to every household in the country, graphically explaining the sudden emergence of the newly discovered, incurable and out-of-control disease, which was threatening the whole of humanity. Primetime television showed dire warnings of what lay ahead for mankind as more and more people became infected and the monster, known as AIDS, permeated through every tier of society. The blame for the rise of the pandemic was laid squarely at the foot of homosexual men, resulting in most people becoming afraid of any form of contact, no matter how remote, with any gay person, or indeed anyone who might have any homosexual tendencies.

Some people even imagined that AIDS could be spread by gay plumbers contaminating water supplies after working on pipes, or that communal swimming pools could become infected by a gay man simply taking a dip. Churchgoers even refused to sip wine during the holy communion ceremony in case there was some closeted gay lurking in the congregation.

My sister Jackie and I went, by train, with Howard to visit the Terrance Higgins Trust, across from Kings Cross Station in London. The trust had been established in the mid-1980s as a charity to provide help and services, such as counselling and health education for people who had contracted HIV/AIDS.

I sat in the waiting room reading my hardback copy of Paul Auster's new book *Moon Palace*, fresh out of Waterstone's and waited for Howard to get through whatever treatment he was receiving.

After spending a few hours at the centre, Howard was feeling relaxed and happy as we left the building to make our way back to his home in Accrington. On the opposite side of the road from the entrance, a small group of protesters had gathered. There was some low-key shouting and waving of placards, displaying signs such as 'Gay men swirl about in a human cesspit of their own making'. (A quote from some high-ranking member of the police force.) And 'Ban gays from public toilets and swimming baths'.

Howard was already showing signs of weakness and frailty and quickly became terrified of the display of hatred demonstrated by the crowd. He wasn't able to hear what they were shouting but he could certainly sense their hostility. My sister and I put our arms around our distressed brother to provide him with some protection and attempted to make our way through the gathering. One particularly aggressive protester moved towards us shouting 'Fucking Homo', with spittle erupting from his mouth. He was much taller than me and powerfully built.

Empowered by the lessons I had been taught during Unarmed Combat training in the Army, the mnemonic SASAS sprang to my mind. Surprise, Aggression, Speed, Accuracy, Strength, all of which are needed for an effective strike. I adopted a submissive stance and cowed as if to accept the man's dominance. As his spit hit my face I used the element of surprise and kicked with all my strength to the side of his knee. He buckled, and as he started to fall towards me I drove the side of my hand aggressively and accurately, as if I were some sort of karate expert, up under the bridge of his nose. I felt the cartilage snap and split under the force, as his face became a mass of blood. With the attacker writhing on the floor I placed my foot across his throat and prepared myself for the next assailant. None came forward. The crowd stood in silence as we walked slowly away from them and towards Euston Station, without any further incident.

There is nothing pretty or fair about Unarmed Combat and there are no niceties such as the Queensbury Rules to prevent permanent injury to the adversaries. Unlike a brawl or a street fight, Unarmed Combat is taught to soldiers to be used ruthlessly and should only ever be considered as a very last resort. Gouging of eyes, snapping of bones and tearing of flesh are all perfectly acceptable as means of survival. In this case, I was wrong to use it, but if I had done as I was taught and used anything available to me as a weapon, in that case, a hardback book, then the assailant could have been killed. I suppose I should have apologised to the foul-mouthed spitting protester – but I didn't.

Over the next two years, Howard's health progressively deteriorated. It was his wish to spend the last part of his life in the Terrance Higgins Trust but he quite suddenly became too ill to travel. He was admitted to the Queens Park Hospital in Blackburn. The doctors made it clear that Howard was dying and was unlikely to survive for more than the next twenty-four hours.

We decided as a family that it would be best if everyone were to say their goodbyes there and then and leave just myself with him till he passed away.

Twenty-four hours went by and, despite huge doses of intravenous diamorphine, Howard was very much alive and able to communicate with me. Over the next six days, he managed to take small amounts of food and water. I cleaned his teeth, brushed his hair and washed him regularly since he had always been fastidious and insisted on being kept clean and tidy. On the final day, Howard told me that his sight was rapidly failing and he was now barely able to see. He was adamant that life trapped in a body without being able to see or hear would be unbearable.

My brother held my hand and begged me to help him.

CHAPTER ONE

I was born and bred, up to the age of seventeen, in Accrington, affectionately known as 'Accy'. Accy was, and still is I think, a grimy industrial town in the north of England. It has a population somewhere in the region of fifty thousand people, being famous only for its football team, 'Accrington Stanley', and its brickworks. The Accrington Brick Company, trade name 'Nori', a contrariwise spelling of Iron was world renowned for the hardness of its bricks, which in 1929 were shipped out to the USA to build the foundations for the Empire State Building.

Growing up was a fairly unremarkable time of my life. I was brought up in what would now be called a slum since we had no bathroom or hot water, and the toilet was one of a block of six old thunder-boxes about twenty yards away from our back door. I never thought it was a slum however, I liked living there, I just didn't like going to the toilet, especially on a cold winters night.

I was never beaten or abused in any way, but I don't remember ever sitting down to a meal with my mum, dad, two older sisters and two younger brothers. My given name was the same as my father's, Patrick James Riley. At the age of four or five dad and mum would sometimes play the game Ludo with myself and my two sisters, which I loved doing.

'I'm red. I'm red!' I would squeal as the Ludo box was being opened.

'OK son, from now on, you are Red.' Said my dad as he patted me on the head affectionately.

The nickname 'Red' has stuck with me to this day, and I am so thankful that I didn't like the colour yellow.

Since regular meals were never a part of my life. As a teenager, I would just grab whatever was available to eat in the kitchen, I was certainly not starved, but I always felt hungry. I remember looking forward to bath time, which would only happen when mum could afford it. Usually once every couple of weeks or so. My mum would give me a towel and a shilling and send me off to the public baths in Accy, with strict instructions to make sure that I washed behind my ears and the back of my neck. I was off like a shot, straight round to the chip shop in Church Street for four penn'eth of chips and a tupenny scallop, which was just a deep-fried slice of potato in greasy batter. Next stop was the corner shop for a selection of their finest Liquorice sticks, halfpenny Spanishes to dip into the two penn'eth of Kaylie; the local name for sherbet, and a pocket full of penny chews and gobstoppers.

I then walked around the town centre, for as long as I reckoned it would take to have a bath. Next stop was the public toilets to wet my face and hair in the sink, not forgetting of course to dampen the towel my mum had given me. Looking back, it seems strange that I would forego the opportunity of a, far from regular, hot bath for the sake of a few sweets.

I left the Holy Family Secondary School in Accrington at the age of fifteen with no qualifications whatsoever. I was scheduled to sit some exams and would, probably, have done quite well in them. However, I decided to give them a miss and go to work helping my dad to plaster a living room ceiling instead, having told him that it was my last term at school, and our whole class had been given the week off. Looking back, it seems likely that the deceptions and lies that I practised as a youngster would give me the inherent qualities necessary to become a successful spy many years later.

It didn't take long for me to get fed up of mixing plaster and making brews for my dad, although I did enjoy being close to him, and I loved his quirky anecdotes, like:

'Time and plaster wait for no man!'

Or: 'If ifs and buts were whisky and nuts, we'd all have a Merry Christmas!'

He was a quiet man with a lovely sense of humour, and I thought he was the best plasterer and dad in the whole world!

One morning I woke up and decided, without talking it over with anyone, that I was going to join the Army. I went down to the phone box at the bottom of the hill where we lived and rummaged through the phone book until I found the address of the nearest Army recruiting office, which happened to be on Station Road, Blackburn. Blackburn was a five-mile walk from home and it was belting it down with rain. Even wet-through, I couldn't have weighed in at much more than six stone, so I must have looked like a drowned rat when I finally arrived to offer my services to Queen and Country.

When I told the recruiting sergeant that I was here to join the Army he looked me up and down for what seemed to be an age and said, "Bugger off and come back when you are old enough t'shave!"

I was gutted, and the pathetic look on my face must have struck a chord with the rugged looking sergeant, for as I turned to leave, and start the long walk back to Accy, his voice had mellowed a little as he told me.

"The minimum age is seventeen and a half, son... I'll still be here when you come back."

And he was.

Two years later, almost to the day, I was there again. I still had another month to go before the minimum age of seventeen years and six months, but I couldn't wait to get away from Accy and begin what I imagined was going to be one big adventure. I should have been sent packing again, but I got the feeling that the grumpy old recruiting sergeant had taken a bit of a liking to me. He told me to take a seat and he allowed me to start the enlistment process, which included sitting the necessary exams, with a view to starting my training the following month, January 1964.

I must have done reasonably well in the exams since I was informed that my results meant that I had qualified not only for one of the most elite branches of the Army, but I was also being recommended to join the Royal Corps of Signals. The Royal Signals is a technical corps responsible for communications throughout the British Army and some parts of the Royal Air Force. It was some years later that I learned that this was total bullshit and it was, in fact, just the luck of the draw, and I was being allocated a place wherever there happened to be a shortage. Even so, the sergeant's flim-flam had worked and I was happy to be offered a place which I readily accepted. I took the option to sign on for the maximum allowable period of twenty-two years, with the first opportunity to leave after nine, mainly because this attracted, by far, the best pay deal of seven pounds and seven shillings a week. With no food or lodgings to pay for, this meant that I would be able to send one pound a week home, put another pound in the Post Office Savings Bank and still afford to live like a lord!

I took the Bible in my right hand and swore allegiance to the queen, and then signed the Official Secrets Act. The signing of the Official Secrets Act was necessary for any potential member of the Royal Signals likely to have access to the country's most secret secrets – bit more bullshit from sergeant nice guy.

Before leaving the recruiting office I was given a railway warrant from

Accrington to Catterick in North Yorkshire, made out for the tenth of January 1964. After handing me one pound seven shillings and sixpence to cover my days' pay and expenses, more than I normally had to last me a week, the recruiting Sergeant shook my hand and welcomed me to "The most noble profession in the world – a soldier in the British Army". Even though I could now afford to take the bus, I chose to walk back to Accy and ponder what lay ahead for me. Upon arriving home, I recall my Mum and Dad seemed to be a bit surprised, almost shocked, at what I had just done, but it didn't take long for them to accept that there was no way they were going to change what I was setting out to do and they soon got used to the idea.

CHAPTER TWO

I arrived in Catterick camp after the longest train journey I had ever taken which had been delayed due to heavy snow over the bleak North Yorkshire Moors. Ahead of me lay six weeks of basic Army training. Having been warned to expect life to be tough, I was pleasantly surprised to find that, not only did I not find it tough, I loved it!

Shortly after I arrived a whole bunch of us raw recruits were lined up and told to undress in preparation for our first medical examination. The Medical Officer came down the line towards me giving each recruit a very brief physical assessment, generating a loud cough from each one in turn.

'Stand up straight, lad!' said the Corporal as the M.O. approached.

He stood in front of me and cast his eyes from head to toe, taking a step backwards and focusing on my feet which, by now, had a few weeks of grime caked on them. I began to wish that I hadn't spent my fortnightly bath money on chips and sweets. I felt fairly certain that I was in for an embarrassing bollocking in front of my newly acquired peers. But it didn't happen. Instead, he stepped forward and whispered in my ear.

"Don't let me see your feet like that again soldier. You know where the showers are – use them."

That M.O. made a lasting impression on me, and I certainly took his advice. From that day forward my feet have been a sight to behold, and getting my shoes and socks off has always been an important part of my courting ritual.

We were certainly kept busy during this introductory period to my life in the army. At five-thirty every morning the silence was shattered by the booming voice of the corporal in charge.

'Reveille! Hands off cocks, Hands on socks. Twenty minutes be standing by your beds, ready for PT!'

After PT, we were kept continuously on the go until lights out at ten o'clock from Monday to Saturday, and on Sunday it was church parade. Church parade was the part of basic training which I disliked the most. It entailed turning out in our best uniforms and being thoroughly inspected by the troop sergeant. We were then marched to the relevant church which catered for the denomination declared on the initial recruitment form. This would either be Church of England or Catholic, since there was no provision to indicate agnostic, atheist or any other religion. For over an hour we were made to stand, or kneel, in front of the padre and mumble the appropriate bits of the service where the congregation are meant to join in. All this chanting was mumbo-jumbo to me since the only times I had ever been in a church was to attend weddings, funerals or christenings.

For the first time in my life, I was being supplied with three good meals a day, which I certainly took advantage of. I gorged myself on everything from black pudding and sausages in the morning to jam roly-poly in the evening. The huge intake of food and the many hours of gruelling physical exercise each day meant that, by the time I got to the end of my basic Army training, I was in superb physical condition. I was still not quite, eighteen years old.

Having qualified as a trained soldier, and being designated the rank of signalman, which is a private really, but signalman sounded marginally better. I was entitled to my first period of leave.

The seventy-two-hour long weekend pass which I was granted, was spent strutting around Accrington in my shiny new boots and uniform and splashing out the small fortune I had saved from my seven pounds seven shillings a week amongst my old, school mates.

Over the next fourteen weeks the Army and, more specifically, the Royal Corps of Signals taught me a trade. At the age of eighteen, not only was I now a trained soldier, but I also became a qualified lineman, which was basically a second, or even a third-rate telephone engineer.

My first posting was to Royal Air Force Station, Laarbruch on the German/Dutch border with the nearest large town being Roermond in Holland.

CHAPTER THREE
MOLLY

It was whilst installing some new telephone equipment into the Officers' Mess that I met the woman who was to become my first wife. She was eighteen at the time and working as the Mess Receptionist. In those days, and perhaps even today, social intercourse between the likes of me, a lowly private in the Army, who wasn't even allowed to enter the Officers Mess via the front door, and the debutante-like young female sitting behind reception, was strictly taboo. Something had to be done if there was to be any chance of me getting to chat with her, and perhaps even showing her my feet. I left the building, via the back door, of course, and drove around to the central telephone exchange. It didn't take me long to locate the circuit for the Officers' Mess reception number and pull out the circuit breaker. All I had to do now was wait.

The telephone operator passed me a message that a fault had occurred, on the phone of the Officers' Mess reception, which looked like a complete disconnection, and I needed to get on to it straight away. A quick splash of Old Spice, a comb through my hair, a check in the mirror and I was back in front of the reception desk. I explained to the damsel in distress, that it may take some time, but I was here to undertake a detailed investigation of the phone, the line, and the connection box under the desk, which was where I felt almost sure the fault lay. After twenty minutes of waiving a screwdriver about and laying on the charm, I rang my mate in the exchange who then popped the circuit breaker back in. Not only had I fixed the fault, which had the desired effect of impressing the nubile receptionist no end, but I also got a pot of tea served on a tray and a cup and saucer with a biscuit the size of a threepenny bit. I also managed to get a date to the camp cinema for the following Friday night, when the film *The Dam Busters*, starring Richard Todd and Michael Redgrave, was being shown. Being on an RAF base, the cinema was bound to be packed out. Getting a seat was going to be difficult enough, let alone getting two together in the back row, which is what I was most certainly aiming for.

15

Her name was Molly and she turned out to be far more than just a reception-
tionist. She was, in fact, the station commander's daughter, no less. Officers
and their families were kept very much apart from the other ranks such as
myself and I knew that I was playing a dangerous game by pursuing her.
Nevertheless, not only did we make the camp cinema that Friday night, with
a bit of a snog and a fumble thrown in, but we started seeing each other regularly. Within a couple of months, she fell pregnant and a few months later
we were married in the registry office in Burnley. My mum and dad were
not only the witnesses at the wedding but were also the only guests, and a
grand reception was held in the chip shop across the road where potato pie,
chips and mushy peas, were served at my dad's expense.

To say that my new, highly esteemed father-in-law, was disappointed in
his daughter's choice of consort would be a huge understatement – he would
probably have described his feelings as 'frightfully displeased' rather than
'pissed off'! He could probably have coped with a son-in-law who fell slightly
short of the standards required of a thrusting young Air Force fighter pilot,
but a private in the Army was almost beyond his comprehension. I fell so
far short of the standards he expected and required for his daughter that he
could barely bring himself to look at me, let alone speak to me. It took a full
two years for him to deign to hold a conversation with me and another two
for him to invite me to his golf club for a round with his chums. I didn't need
to think too long and hard about his invitation. I just always seemed to be
far too busy to accept.

Having been blessed with eyes like a shit-house rat I turned out to be
a very good marksman. I was selected to represent the Corps in shooting
competitions across Germany and Holland and each year went back to the
United Kingdom to take part in the National Championships in Bisley,
home of the NRA – the National Rifle Association – just outside London.

Apart from fixing phones and shooting, I was also making up for the lost
time at school by going to night classes to get my qualifications in maths,
English, physics and the like.

Every working day, orders and notices were posted outside the troop
office and it was whilst reading them one evening in July 1970 that my life
took on a whole new direction.

Volunteers required to train as Army Pilots was the headline on the notice
board.

CHAPTER FOUR

The Army pilot's course is one of the toughest courses in the Army to get through. It consisted of an initial selection phase at the Officer and Aircrew Selection Centre (OASC) at RAF Biggin Hill. If successful at the OASC then candidates would progress to a further selection phase at the Army Air Corps Centre at Middle Wallop in Hampshire. Then came the biggest test of all, the pilot's course proper, which consisted of a full twelve months of intensive flying training and ground school covering the technical and tactical aspects of flying as an operational pilot.

I received notification that my application to volunteer for the course had been accepted and I was ordered to attend the first phase of the selection process in March 1971. I had no idea then how slim my chances of getting over even the first hurdle were. Less than fifty percent of candidates make it through the Officer and Aircrew Selection process, most failing on medical grounds such as; eye muscle balance tests, colour perception, or even having shin bones that are over the maximum allowable length for sitting in a military cockpit. All these conditions were unlikely to have had any impact upon an individual prior to the medical examination, and usually came as a shock to the candidate before being sent packing and graded as medically unfit to serve as aircrew. Next came a whole raft of tests from progressive matriculations to mechanical comprehension and complicated coordination appraisals to get through. Having passed the OASC, I was then on my way to Middle Wallop, deep in the Hampshire countryside, for the more practical aspects of the assessment, such as military organisation and the ability to take command and control in a wartime environment. Part of the test was 'Signals', which covered details of communications, not just within the Army, but throughout the military as a whole. A subject in which I was expected to excel, being a fully paid-up member of the elite Royal Corps of Signals. As it turned out I gained the very dubious distinction of becoming the first ever member of the Corps to fail the 'Signals' exam. The testing officers seemed to be dumbfounded and had difficulty understanding how I could have failed the test since they assumed that my knowledge of communications must have been vastly superior even to theirs. Rather than giving me the boot there and then, they agreed that I should be allowed to re-sit the exam the following day. I decided that I was not going to take any chances. The only way I was going to guarantee passing was to take up smoking!

In those days, it was quite acceptable to smoke in classrooms, so the following morning I popped around to the NAAFI store and bought myself twenty Embassy filter-tipped cigarettes and a box of Swan Vesta matches, they were in the largest packets I could find, and size was going to be important. In the tiniest of manuscript, I wrote as many facts and cribs as I could on the insides of the packets. Only by lighting up fag after fag and studiously gazing into the cigarette packet and match box was I able to pass the exam, and subsequently the whole Pilot Selection process. I was lucky, and I succeeded only by the skin of my teeth and, of course, resorting to rather unethical methods.

It was then that I adopted the mantra, 'Win if you can. Lose if you must. But cheat at all costs!'

CHAPTER FIVE

In November 1972, I started my pilot's course. I had hardly any problems with the flying side of the course, and what troubles I did have with the ground school were easily overcome with the occasional packet of Embassy filter tips. Out of the initial intake of twenty-two that started the course, a total of seven students made it through to the Wings Parade. Throughout the twelve months of training, there was very little leeway given to anyone not achieving the required flying standards on target, and the course gradually diminished in size. One poor bugger got the chop on the very last day of the course! At the Wings Parade, not only did my parents and wife attend, but I was also honoured to have the presence of my illustrious father-in-law. I couldn't be certain, but he did seem to be almost beaming with pride as His Royal Highness, Prince Phillip, stuck the Army Flying Wings on to my chest, and he made a big effort to muscle his way into the conversation between the prince and I during drinks after the parade.

Over the next three years, I consolidated my flying skills and my annual flying assessment improved from 'proficient' to 'average' then 'high average' and eventually 'above average', the highest grade of evaluation it was realistically possible to achieve.

I completed operational tours of duty in Northern Ireland, jungle flying in Belize and Brunei, and Arctic warfare training in Norway. I flew in the deserts of Oman and the vast prairies of Southern Canada. At least once a year I took part in mountain flying in the Alps, the Pyrenees or the Troodos mountains of Cyprus.

By now, I was considered to be a very experienced and competent military pilot who could be deployed with confidence to any part of the world. After an interview with the Army Air Corps Senior Flying Examiner, I was strongly recommended to become an instructor and was subsequently allocated a slot at the Central Flying School in the summer of 1979. But instructing was not what I wanted to do. I had my sights on, what I considered to be, the best job in the British Army – the flight commander of the Special Air Service Flight in Hereford.

And there was every chance I could get the job since I was sufficiently well qualified and my flying assessment was as good as you could get. Everything was looking good as far as my career was concerned. Only an almighty fuck-up could, not only put my chances of wrangling the plum job I so desired in jeopardy, but also risk me being stripped of my flying status and sent back to The Royal Signals – and an almighty fuck-up it really was!

It was during a very simple task in the UK that things suddenly started to go wrong and my career was about to take a nosedive.

CHAPTER SIX

Running out of fuel in a military aircraft is a serious offence and no excuses whatsoever can be tolerated. Any pilot who runs out of fuel and survives can expect to be permanently grounded at the very least, and thrown out of the Army in disgrace as a more likely outcome.

I was based in Netheravon, Wiltshire when I was given a very straightforward task – pick up two passengers from London Battersea Heliport and drop them off at the United Kingdom Land Forces Headquarters in Wilton near Salisbury.

The forecast weather chart indicated extensive fog across the southern part of the country, which was expected to hang around until late afternoon. Fog is only a problem for a helicopter when taking-off and landing. It tends to be only a few hundred feet thick, so my plan was to fly at about two thousand feet to stay well clear of the top of it. All I needed to do was to confirm that Battersea was not fogbound and I could be on my way. I rang the Heliport in London and Barbara, the air traffic controller of the day confirmed that, from where she was sitting, the weather looked perfect; clear blue sky and very little breeze. She also stressed that she was very much looking forward to seeing me since we had been having an affair for some months; an affair which was destined to continue over the next five years.

I took on only enough fuel to get to the Heliport since I was determined not to waste time refuelling. Instead, I decided that it would be a nice idea to get there well before the passengers, in order for me to spend as much time as possible with the new love of my life. Having got confirmation from Barbara that the weather was clear I considered that it was a pretty safe bet that it was unlikely to deteriorate over the next hour or two, so I was good to go. Someone with my flying experience should have appreciated that occasionally the weather deviates from the script on the forecast. Bad weather has a habit of catching nonchalant pilots off their guard. On this particular day, I would have been far better off spending a little more time taking on fuel and less time thinking about how I might impress the air traffic controller.

I climbed away from Netheravon and levelled off at fifteen hundred feet, well clear of the top of the cloud. With an estimated time on route of fifty minutes, and about seventy minutes' fuel on board I would be on the ground at Battersea in plenty of time for me to order a refuel and sit in the tower for an hour or so laying on the charm – I might even get a chance to take my flying boots off!

The forecast was right. The fog was very extensive and I could see nothing of the ground. The smoke rising from the Didcot Power Station and the top of the Stokenchurch television mast sticking up through the sea of white were the only visible landmarks I had. As I approached London Heathrow controlled airspace I was still unable to see anything but fog in any direction. Listening in to the air traffic radio it seemed to be unusually quiet for that time of day.

"Heathrow this is Army two four zero, request clearance to enter controlled airspace inbound to Battersea Heliport. Over," I transmitted.

"Army two four zero this is Heathrow; Battersea is closed due to dense fog. Over," came the reply.

'Bollocks,' I muttered to myself. 'Only twenty minutes of fuel left at the most, and nothing but dense fog in every direction.'

"Roger that," I replied as calmly as I could manage. "Can you tell me the nearest airfield that is clear? Over."

"Birmingham is the nearest diversion but Oxford are just reporting an improvement with six hundred metres visibility."

"Roger. Diverting to Oxford," I said, as I started a steep turn back towards the west.

I couldn't possibly make Birmingham but I had a reasonable chance of making it to Oxford, and, even though the visibility there was far from good, it was my only realistic option. With five miles to run the fog was breaking and I was getting occasional glimpses of the ground.

With two miles to run the cockpit burst into life with warning lights and audio alarms as the engine, starved of fuel, flamed-out. I immediately pressed the radio transmit button.

"Mayday, Mayday! Army two four zero engine failure two miles east of Oxford forced landing!"

By pure chance, I was directly over an open field and I carried out a perfect engine-off landing, something I had practised many times during training but this was my first one in earnest.

Now I had to think quickly if I were to avoid facing disciplinary action and, at the very least, the sack. Sitting in silence in a misty field, I made my next transmission which I hoped would save my career.

"Oxford, Army two four zero cancel Mayday. I had a spurious warning and I intend to make a precautionary landing and get things checked by speaking to engineering once I have landed. Over."

"Roger," came the reply. "Mayday is cancelled. Give us a call on the land-line once you are safely on the ground if you need any assistance. Over."

I breathed a sigh of relief as I wandered over to the nearby farmhouse. But my deception was far from over and I realised that I still had a fair bit of work to do before I could relax.

I told the friendly farmer that I had had a problem with my fuel gauge and that I intended to pick up a few gallons of diesel from the nearest garage, just to get me over to the adjacent airfield, which was now clearly visible as the weather continued to improve. The farmer couldn't have been more helpful. He went into his barn, dusted the straw and cobwebs off a couple of old Jerry Cans and threw them into the back of his tractor. He then drove me down to the local garage where I filled up the cans. Once we were back at the helicopter he even held the funnel for me as I filled up with enough diesel to get me over the fence to the airfield refuel facility.

Upon arrival, back at base, I reported to Operations that the passengers had resorted to road transport due to the extensive fog, and the inaccuracy of the weather forecast.

"By the way," I said, "during the sortie, I had developed a fault with the fuel gauge, which had required me to make an unscheduled landing". (Not too far from the truth I suppose.)

I also made it clear that I would be completing a detailed report of the possible defect to the engineering officer.

Tom was the chief engineer on duty that day, which was great since we got on well together. We were long-term friends and had both recently been promoted from sergeant to staff sergeant. The celebration drinks in the Station Sergeants' Mess had started after lunch and continued until well after breakfast time the next day. I explained to Tom that the fuel gauge had got stuck when indicating about twenty minutes' endurance remaining.

This had caused me concern since I felt uncertain as to whether I may be about to run out of fuel, and I had considered it prudent to land, just as a precaution. (That was definitely, quite a long way short of the truth). Tom fell for it hook, line and sinker and decided that the incident had serious flight safety implications. He was genuinely concerned and said that he intended to recommend that the fuel gauges across the whole fleet, regardless of where they were in the world, should be checked immediately.

A few weeks later I was summoned to the commanding officer's office. Being invited to the C.O.'s office for an interview was a little out of the ordinary. The commanding officer of a regiment, which generally consists of four squadrons, would hold the rank of lieutenant colonel. As a staff sergeant, subject to any disciplinary action, I would, under normal circumstances, be required to appear before my squadron commander who would hold the lesser rank of major.

The fact that I was being ordered to circumvent the established chain of command didn't bode well and I had to admit to being more than a little worried. I really didn't cherish the thought of being sent back to the Royal Corps of Signals as a corporal or, worse still, joining the dole queue back in Accrington.

'Good morning, staff,' said the C.O. as I stood to attention in front of his desk. 'Please take a seat and relax. There are three things that I would like to talk to you about today,' he said, as he began thumbing through the paperwork on his desk.

Fuck! Don't tell me he knows about Barbara, and the ration storeman's wife, as well as the fuel-gauge fiasco, I thought to myself.

"Firstly. regarding the situation with the fuel gauges, I can tell you that every single unit across the fleet has now been checked. Thanks to your diligence and professionalism, several faults have been found, and it is my considered opinion that your actions could have saved at least one, and possibly more, potential accidents. I would like you to accept this as a formal commendation which will be included in your record of service. Very well done indeed."

I was speechless.

"Secondly, as from now I will no longer refer to you as 'staff' but will be addressing you as Mister Riley, since you are forthwith promoted to the rank of warrant officer. Many congratulations."

I was gob-smacked. What the fuck could be coming next? Surely, he couldn't be about to tell me that I had come up on the Littlewoods Pools, but then again, the way things were going why not?

I hadn't won the Pools, but what he did tell me was even better. My course at the Army's Central Flying School had been cancelled and I was to be appointed as the flight commander of the Special Air Service flight in Hereford as from November 1979.

Getting away with running out of fuel came as a huge and pleasant surprise. Being commended, promoted, and given the best job in the Army all on the same day called for an outrageous celebration in the warrant officers and sergeants mess. It was made even more outrageous when I was joined by Tom, the engineer, who had also received a commendation for his professional conduct and been told that he was to be promoted later that month.

Anyone thinking that I had been extremely lucky and would be wise to tread carefully, and apply myself to my new job with measured professionalism and dedication would be absolutely right.

Anyone thinking that that was what I was about to do would be absolutely wrong.

CHAPTER SEVEN

Strict radio silence has been imposed, which is normal just prior to a planned assault. The elements of surprise and timing are vital and radio silence must only be broken if any member of the team comes under direct attack from the enemy. Otherwise, the next voice we hear will be the operational commander. He alone will decide when the strike will be launched.

We wait in silence, like coiled springs, only the breathing of the five of us on board the helicopter can be heard over the aircraft intercom. We are on the ground, a little over a mile from the Embassy building, which we are about to attack with as much fire power and force as is necessary to save the hostages. It has been drummed into every member of the team, time and again, that the aim is not to kill the terrorists, it is 'To save the hostages'. Always said twice for maximum emphasis, 'To save the hostages.'

We are part of the United Kingdom Counter-Terrorist Team based in Bradbury Lines, Hereford, and have been tasked to deal with an ongoing hostage situation in the Embassy building just seconds away from our location.

As the pilot, my job is simply to deliver the four members of the assault team onto the Embassy roof as quickly as possible after the order 'Go Go Go' is given. The SAS team members are standing on the skids on the outside of the aircraft. Short ropes with quick-release devices are attached from their waistbands to the helicopter cargo hooks acting as umbilicals. Dressed completely in black, they are carrying Heckler and Koch MP5 submachine guns. Their chests and belts are dripping with an assortment of explosives and grenades. Respirators are strapped to their heads, ready to drop into place over their mouths once the attack gets underway. Respirators are necessary so as not to be overcome by the debilitating gas released from the stun grenades which will be used as an opening gambit.

A minute passes but it seems to be an awful lot longer.

'Standby,' says the commander almost in a whisper.

The tension on board now becomes palpable.

I raise the collective control lever with my left hand just enough to start to break contact with the ground. The guys on the skids drop their respirators into place in almost perfect unison.

"Go Go Go!" shouts the commander.

We are up from behind cover in an instant, like a cork out of a bottle. I pull as much power as I can without over-torqueing the gearbox and ram the cyclic control forward to gain as much speed as possible.

A huge explosion erupts from the front of the Embassy building and we disappear into the billowing smoke. Only metres to go now so, getting only intermittent glimpses of the rooftops, I flare the aircraft to slow down by pulling back on the cyclic and reducing power. It's as if I have flown into the middle of a New Year's Eve fireworks display and I have to concentrate intently on focusing on the Embassy roof, the chimney-stacks and the array of aerials.

Less than forty seconds after take-off, I establish a four-foot hover and the guys leap off the skids, tossing stun grenades as they go. The intense flashes of light given off by the grenades is intended to disorientate the enemy, and it's only with intense concentration that I manage to lift off safely, and fly away from the mayhem.

The training exercise is over and back at base we discuss the finer points of what went wrong and what went right, when we stormed the purpose-built Embassy building in our training facility, in Pontrilas Army Training Area, just outside Hereford.

In my new role as commander of the Special Air Service Flight my responsibility was to provide helicopter support for the UK Counter-Terrorist Team, usually referred to as the S.P. Team. We spent most of our working days developing and practising tactics to deal with the ever-present threat of national and international terrorism. Repeatedly we rehearsed storming buildings, planes, buses, trains and ships alongside. Ships that were not alongside, in other words out at sea, were the responsibility of the Royal Marines Special Boat Service who were based in Poole in Dorset.

Generally, the function of the helicopters was to transport the command element of the S.P. Team to the scene of the incident as quickly as possible. A secondary role was to deliver members of the assault section of the team directly on to the target once the order to attack had been received.

We practised a wide range of methods of delivery; from approaching to a low hover and the team members simply leaping off the skids, to fast roping, abseiling and free fall parachuting. All these techniques had to be mastered by day or night, with or without lights, and in pretty much, all weather conditions.

Throughout the year, we had a constant stream of visitors from the forty-five police constabularies of the UK to politicians and Royalty, all expecting to see a dramatic demonstration of how we would deal with, just about, any hostage situation.

When Prince Charles and Lady Diana visited, the exercise was made more interesting than usual when Lady Di got too close to the action and her hair caught fire. The prince flew with me as we demonstrated storming an aircraft, and I then asked him if he would like to take the flying controls for the next part of the exercise which was assailing of the Embassy building.

"Well I would love to, but I'm afraid I don't have my flying gloves with me," said the prince.

"Don't worry sir you can borrow mine," I said, "This could be your claim to fame. One day you will be able to tell people that you once wore 'Red' the Pilot's flying gloves."

This sent a ripple of laughter around the royal entourage including Lady Di who was giving me, what could only be described as a 'smouldering' look. Unfortunately, there was no sexual aspiration to the look, it was just that her hair was still smoking slightly.

The future king did take control of the aircraft and he flew very well until we were in the middle of the 'fireworks display', when I thought it might be prudent to help him out just a little. Our demonstrations invariably went down very well with the hierarchy, although they did tend to interrupt our rigorous training regime.

There is an old military adage – 'Train hard fight easy', and train hard is exactly what we did.

CHAPTER EIGHT
OPERATION NIMROD

As a group, we trained in anticipation of coming up against hardened and ruthless terrorists. We found it easy to convince ourselves that it was only a matter of time before a major hostage situation would develop somewhere on UK soil.

The last time the regiment had been involved in a real hostage incident had been the Balcombe Street siege, back in 1975. After carrying out several murderous bombing attacks across England, four members of an IRA active service unit took two members of the public hostage after being cornered by police in a flat in Balcombe Street, Marylebone, London. Throughout the six days of the siege the SP team planned and rehearsed attacks on the building where the hostages were being held. The gunmen eventually surrendered to police before any strike was carried out, and the IRA men were later charged with ten murders and twenty bombings. All of them were jailed for life.

Almost five years later, in April 1980, six armed men burst into the Iranian Embassy on Princes Gate, South Kensington, London, and took control of the building. They held twenty-six people, including one police officer who had been on duty guarding the Embassy, as hostages. The attackers claimed to be members of a little-known Iranian Arab group, formed to protest against the oppression of Khuzestan by the Iranian leader Ayatollah Khomeini.

Within minutes of the siege becoming established, SAS Group Headquarters on the Kings Road in Chelsea had been alerted and they, in turn, had ordered the SP team in Bradbury Lines to come to immediate readiness and prepare to move. In houses, pubs and clubs across the small rural town of Hereford, the SP team members' personal bleepers flashed, indicating that this was not an exercise but a potential operation and to get into camp and be ready to move as quickly as possible.

Less than thirty minutes after receiving the call-out I was airborne with the Counter Terrorist Command team on board, en route to Regents Park Barracks, which was a stone's throw away from the besieged Iranian Embassy.

For the transit, I didn't use my normal 'Army two four zero' call sign but instead adopted 'Doughnut Sierra', a call sign allocated to me which was only to be used when genuine threats to national security had been declared. Air traffic control services across the country had routinely been instructed to give any 'Doughnut' call sign absolute priority over all other traffic apart from an immediate life-threatening emergency.

After landing at Regents Park, preparations prior to the arrival of the rest of the team had to be organised without delay. The carparking area had to be cleared to make room for a further one, and possibly two, more helicopters. There was also a whole convoy of SP team vehicles including Range Rovers, transit vans, pantechnicons and a fifty-six-seater bus barrelling down the M4 motorway towards London. The bus, already prepared and equipped with covert microphones and cameras, was also fitted with remotely detonated stun grenades and gas producers which could be used if the vehicle were to be stormed.

A Command and Control Centre needed to be established. Basic accommodation with catering facilities for up to one hundred men would also be required. The building which had the largest open space was the gymnasium and this needed to be completely cleared for a team of Royal Pioneer Corps carpenters to supervise the building of a facsimile of the room layout of the Embassy, for the assault teams to practice room to room clearance.

Upon arrival of the team, our priority would be to implement an Immediate Action plan. An IA would be necessary in case negotiations broke down, and the situation became rapidly out of control. Should the operational commander consider it likely that the terrorists were about to start killing the hostages, then the IA drill would be initiated.

A much-preferred option to an IA was a Deliberate Action, which would normally take a considerable amount of time to prepare. The team needed to gain access to the adjacent buildings, put together bespoke frame charges and other explosive devices. They also needed to identify entry points and solid anchors to secure abseil ropes. Perhaps most importantly, they needed to obtain detailed plans of the building, in order to reconstruct the layout to practise room clearances and allocate areas of responsibility for each assault team member.

The IA plan, which included one helicopter at the front and one at the back delivering the assault teams on to the roof, would remain extant only until the Deliberate Action was considered to be adequately prepared. This turned out to be a full two days into the operation.

It wasn't until lunchtime on the sixth day of the siege that the situation quickly began to spiral out of control. Negotiations between the police and the hostage takers had started breaking down and when three shots were heard from inside the building, everyone in the control room started to fear the worst.

At about seven o'clock that evening a body was thrown out of the front door of the embassy and the terrorists threatened to kill one hostage every half hour.

The senior police officer on duty, who would not normally be below the rank of chief superintendent, was in total control of the situation. He would only hand control over to the senior Army commander if he considered that the lives of the hostages were in imminent danger, and military action had become unavoidable. The terrorists had now crossed the line and, believing that any further negotiations would be futile, the chief constable handed over control to the military. Operation Nimrod was declared active, and it was about to get very interesting indeed.

Upon receipt of the 'Go Go Go' from the commander, several teams would attempt to enter the building at, exactly the same time. All with the unambiguous aim of 'saving the hostages'.

By this time the Deliberate Action had been developed and refined with everything, and everyone, ready to move into position to assault the embassy, and formal control was accepted by Lieutenant Colonel Mike Rose, the Senior Military Representative. The operational commander instructed the teams to move, as silently as possible, to their start positions, and check in when ready to launch the coordinated and simultaneous attack.

The police negotiators were asked to keep the lead hostage-taker, Awn Ali Mohammed, known as Salim, as busy as possible on the phone. One team was standing by, on the roof, ready to lower an explosive device down through the skylight and enter the building via the stairway. A second team, with prepared Explosive Frame Charges, would attach them to the first-floor windows, approaching from the balcony next door. Teams positioned in the rear garden would blow out the patio doors to gain access to clear the basement and the ground floor.

As the remaining teams were abseiling into positions on the second- and first-floor rear balconies, one of the team smashed a window with his foot. Salim was immediately alerted and, becoming very agitated, slammed the phone down on the negotiator. The commander instantly decided that the element of total surprise had been lost and transmitted 'Go Go Go'.

Seconds later a tremendous explosion shook the whole of number 16 Princes Gate, as the rooftop team lowered their explosive charge down through the central skylight. Almost simultaneously, the team on the first-floor balcony detonated their prepared frame charges, and a huge plume of smoke enshrouded the front of the building. Watched by millions of television viewers around the world, a team burst through the smoke and into the first-floor library. The first hostage to be encountered was a BBC sound engineer, Sim Harris, who was unceremoniously grabbed and shoved out onto the balcony, where he then crossed to the safety of the National School of Needlework next door. The library was quickly cleared and, as the team moved through the building, a gunman who was attempting to escape into a room off the corridor they were in, was shot dead.

Meanwhile, Salim, the lead hostage-taker, ran towards the first-floor window brandishing his semi-automatic AK47 rifle. The police officer, who had been guarding the embassy as it was taken, Constable Trevor Locke, had managed to keep his pistol hidden throughout the past five days of the siege. Constable Locke dived onto Salim, drawing his weapon at the same time. As the two men wrestled on the floor, the SAS team entered the room. One of them shouted to Locke to roll clear before firing a burst, from his MP5 submachine gun, killing the gang leader instantly.

At the same time, in the communications room on the third floor, the hostages were ordered to sit with their hands on their heads. Realising that they were under attack the terrorists panicked and began indiscriminately firing at the helpless hostages, killing one and seriously wounding a second. Knowing that the assault team were about to enter the room the killers panicked, threw their weapons to one side and attempted to hide amongst the hostages, but the ruse didn't work and they were quickly identified and shot dead.

Thinking that all the hostages were now safe, the team lined them up and started to marshal them into the back garden via the central staircase. Halfway down the stairs, a team member identified a terrorist who was holding a hand grenade. Unable to open fire because of the people around him, the soldier smashed him in the face with the butt of his weapon instead. The grenade flew out of the man's hand, fortunately not exploding. He rolled, semi-conscious, to the bottom of the stairs where he was met by a volley of machine gun fire, ending his days of being a hero of Khuzestan, or anywhere else for that matter.

Having reached the garden, the hostages were made to lie face down and their hands were handcuffed behind their backs. Five of the DRFA group were now dead but one was still unaccounted for. It was then that Sim Harris, the BBC man pointed out that Fawaz Nijad, the last of the group was, in fact, lying on the ground masquerading as a hostage. Nijad was dragged away and handed over to the police. He was eventually charged with murder and sentenced to life imprisonment.

With all the hostages now safe, five terrorists dead and one in custody, control was handed back to the police and Operation Nimrod was coming to an end.

We all gathered in the dining hall jostling and barging to get a good view of the television, which had been set up for us to watch the BBC news, which was due to start shortly. Just as the opening music for the news was playing I received a message, *'Casevac request immediate'.* I was a bit disgruntled that I would miss the dramatic events unfolding on TV but, having just received a new, state of the art, VHS recorder I knew that I would, at least, be able to watch it later. As I approached the door to leave, in walked the commanding officer, Mike Rose, and Margaret Thatcher, the prime minister, who I almost bumped into.

'This is Red, a member of the team,' said the C.O.

Despite my attempts to avoid her clutches, Mrs Thatcher then flung her arms around me and proceeded to give me a big kiss. I managed to extricate myself from her enthusiastic embrace, whilst the rest of team concentrated on watching their performance on the news, totally ignoring the prime minister. I had the CASEVAC to deal with, which I assumed must be a life-threatening emergency since the nearest hospital was only minutes away by ambulance.

A CASEVAC is a casualty evacuation request normally requiring one, or more, casualties to be extracted from the scene of an accident or incident and taken to the nearest hospital. But this request was unusual. It specified one casualty to be moved from the front of the Iranian Embassy and taken to the Queen Alexandra's Royal Military Hospital just outside Wroughton in Wiltshire, which was exclusively for the use of military personnel. I figured that the casualty had to be Tom, a friend of mine, who had been badly burnt whilst abseiling down the back of the building. His abseil rope had become entangled just above the window through which he was planning to enter the building. The curtains below him were ablaze and Tom was being roasted alive. Only the quick action of a team member saved him by cutting through the rope and deposited Tom into the back garden like a bundle of dirty washing.

Being now in total darkness I asked for the grassed area across from the embassy to be illuminated by the headlights of two vehicles. A standard procedure for a night pick-up, which I felt confident the guys on the ground would be familiar with. I was expecting a stretcher, but as I landed, the back door flew open and in jumped Tom, smelling like a recently extinguished bonfire. A casualty would normally be chaperoned by a medic but as the medic attempted to get on board Tom pushed him away and slammed the door shut. "Right mate let's go," he said. "Forget the hospital, straight back to aitch."

The Royal Air Force Hospital at Wroughton was on the way back to Hereford and over the next few minutes, I managed to convince Tom that we should land there and get him some treatment. It was, a pretty safe bet, that a medical team would be waiting to receive him and we would both be in for a bollocking if we were to stand them up. He agreed, but only if I promised to wait for him for up to an hour, since he made it perfectly clear that he had no intentions of missing the inevitable piss-up about to get underway back at 'aitch' as he called our base in Hereford.

After about forty minutes an apparition emerged from the darkness. With the light behind the apparition I could only make out its teeth and the whites of its eyes but I had no doubt whatsoever, it was Tom. He was wearing a blue and white sleeveless hospital gown and carrying a drip stand with a saline drip inserted into his right arm. The doctors and nurses standing at the hospital entrance had obviously given up and made no attempt to stop the, undoubtedly insane Fijian warrior from having his way and getting back for the piss-up.

We roared with laughter in the euphoric atmosphere of the Officers' Mess that night and I honestly don't remember what time I got to bed.

I loved my job, which I felt confident was secure for, at least, the next three years. Only if I made a horrendous cock-up would my time with the Special Air Service be cut short by the threat of an involuntary RTU. Return to Unit was something to be avoided at all costs. For any member of the Special Forces to be obliged to go back to their parent unit, and then have their records endorsed with 'Services no longer required', was, at that time, considered to be the ultimate disgrace.

CHAPTER NINE

By this time, I was a happily married man with three children and living in a pleasant, four-bedroomed house, in the rural village of Moreton-on-Lugg, five miles north of Hereford.

My father-in-law had recently retired from the Royal Air Force and had now risen through the ranks at the local golf club to become president, no less. Over time, his perception of me had changed somewhat, and I was now considered to be far more socially acceptable. His daughter and I were regularly honoured with invites to lavish functions at the president's table. Functions we were, perhaps predictably, never able to attend.

My dedication to my work meant that I spent far more time away from my family than I needed to. I would be the first to admit that my performance as a husband and father certainly didn't compare to that of my flying ability. 'Proficient' would have been a rather more generous assessment than I deserved. I was still having the affair with Barbara and flew down to Battersea to spend time with her whenever the opportunity arose. My good friend Crocker, Major Crocker, the second-in-command of the regiment at that time, was also having an affair with a woman from London. We would often conspire together, over a brew in his office, to concoct excuses for us to visit Group Headquarters in Chelsea, a visit which could not possibly be done by train or car and would, invariably, involve an overnight stay. If we couldn't think of any good reason for staying overnight then I could always resort to the 'bad weather grounding us till daylight' option, or even affecting a technical fault that would take some time to resolve. The guys back at the Flight in Hereford soon got to know that once the second-in-command and I had departed for London there was no way we would be back before the next day. Crocker's mistress had her own flat in Kensington but Barbara was married to an inspector in the Metropolitan Police so we would usually spend the night, or at least part of it, at the Special Forces club.

The Special Forces Club is a private members club in Knightsbridge just around the corner from Harrods, the world-famous department store. Despite its name, the club has very few members who have ever served with any Special Forces, most qualify for membership instead because of their parents' wartime exploits, or some vague connection with intelligence organisations. The club had only about ten bedrooms which were, more often than not, fully occupied. I had been a member for a few years and had become very friendly with Jenny, the manageress at the time. Jenny would always do her best to fit me in, and often rang me to tell me that she had only one room left, but would keep it available for me for as long as she could. Knowing that Barbara and I were normally pretty desperate, Jenny would often make up a temporary bed for us in the library, putting a 'Closed for Maintenance' notice on the door and locking us in for privacy, until I rang for a taxi to take Barbara home.

Back at base we continued to prepare and train for the next terrorist incident regardless of the argument that, because of the decisive action that was recently taken during Operation Nimrod, another siege involving the taking of hostages, was unlikely to happen again, anywhere in the UK.

We did get some free time, however. Having the luxury of three dedicated pilots I could organise a weekly flying roster. In blocks of seven days, one pilot would be on half hour standby, the second on four hours, and the third would be completely off duty for a week. Even during my weeks off, I would be on camp playing squash, running for miles on end, or free fall parachuting.

Every Wednesday morning at ten-thirty I would have to attend 'prayers'. Prayers was a meeting of all Heads of Departments to discuss problems together and receive briefings and updates on any potential threats and ongoing operations. Regardless of whether I was rostered to be on duty or not, I would always attend prayers.

It was a Friday night in the Sergeant's Mess of 22 SAS, what we often referred to as the most exclusive club in the world, that we were celebrating another promotion. Mick Shearer had just been promoted from warrant officer to captain when, with the celebration barely underway, Mick stunned everyone present by saying that he had to leave. It was a Friday evening and he said he needed to be in Gütersloh, in Germany, no later than Sunday afternoon. The only way he could make it was to get the evening train to London via Bristol and then a very early flight out of Heathrow on Saturday morning.

It was then that I came up with one of my, by now almost famous, ideas – not the brightest one I had ever come up with, as it later transpired. There was a spare helicopter in the hangar and, being a weekend, there would be very few people about. I was off duty for the whole of the following week so, as long as I could be around for Wednesday morning prayers then, I was unlikely to be missed by anyone, if I decided to go away for a few days. I reckoned I would have plenty of time to drop Mick off in Gütersloh and be back in Hereford by Sunday afternoon. Even if the weather turned against us we would be back by Tuesday, at the very latest, and we would be able to pick up a stack of duty-free booze and cigarettes as a bonus. The new captain readily accepted my offer and declared that the drinks were on him for the rest of the evening.

CHAPTER TEN

It was close to one o'clock the following day before the hangover had subsided sufficiently for me to lift off for a planned refuel stop at Lydd Airport in Kent. On board with me were two Micks. Mick, the new captain and Mick the aircraft engineer who had agreed to come along, mainly to keep me company on the return journey. Engineer Mick would also be needed to help me load up the large amounts of contraband we were going to pick up from the duty-free store in the Royal Air Force station at Gütersloh. What wine and spirits we didn't drink we planned to sell, along with the cigarettes, and finish up by making a handsome profit.

It was a beautiful summer's day as we took off from the east coast after refuelling. We crossed the English Channel and coasted in abeam Le Touquet in Continental Europe. Shortly after transiting France and entering Dutch airspace, I noticed that things were not quite right. I was having to progressively apply more collective pitch than was normal, almost certainly meaning that the engine was not producing the optimum amount of power. The engine oil pressure was gradually decreasing and the oil temperature starting to rise. There was little doubt in my mind as to what was going wrong. All the indications were pointing towards an imminent engine failure. I looked across at 'Engineer Mick' and pointed towards the instrument panel. After studying the instruments for a few seconds, he looked back at me with a frown on his face and shook his head slowly. He didn't say anything. He didn't need to. We both knew that we had to land without delay or risk falling out of the sky.

The Royal Netherlands Airforce base of Deelen was about five miles off to our port side. I selected the international distress frequency of 121.5 Mega Hertz and transmitted. "Pan Pan Pan, Deelen this is British Army two four zero, Imminent engine failure, request clearance to land immediately." A 'Pan' call is an urgent message rather than a 'Mayday' call which would indicate a dire emergency. "Roger, British Army two four zero, you are cleared to land directly on the main runway," came the reply.

The engine continued to run, albeit with diminishing power, until we were safely on the ground. But the oil pressure was by then seriously low and I decided to close the engine down without carrying out the normal run-down procedures in an attempt to minimise any further damage.

Before any military aircraft can land in a foreign country, diplomatic clearance must be applied for and granted. I, of course, had no such clearance to land. There was now every chance that my unauthorised entry into Holland was going to be reported, via the British Embassy, to the Foreign and Commonwealth Office, and a complete shit-storm was going to descend upon me.

The fact that we were all in civilian clothes certainly didn't help matters at all, since that left us wide open to being arrested as spies. Despite Captain Mick now being a higher rank than me, it fell on my shoulders, being the aircraft commander, to try to talk our way out of the politically embarrassing situation.

I decided that I would have to play the NATO card, which would allow me to focus on the fact that the United Kingdom and Holland were close allies. Both of us facing up to the nasty Russian hordes preparing, right now, to come storming across the river Rhine. I explained that since we were merely transiting through Dutch airspace, I hadn't considered it necessary to acquire diplomatic clearance. The exercise we were taking part in required us to be dressed in civilian clothes and that if we could just be allowed to contact our unit in Germany, then we could arrange transport and be on our way.

The airforce officers formed a huddle and began chattering away in their native tongue. Despite not understanding a word of Dutch I found it impossible to stop myself from eavesdropping. I managed to pick up the words 'leugenaar' and 'spionnen' which sounded very much to me like 'lying spies', leading me to the conclusion that our troubles were about to get worse. But the old blarney must have had the desired effect. We, or at least I, was still going to be in trouble, but when the senior officer approached us with a smile I felt certain we were not going to be arrested. He not only offered us any assistance we might require, including accommodation, but he also invited us to dine with them once we had made the necessary arrangements to be picked up, enabling us to carry on with our very important work on behalf of NATO.

I rang the commanding officer of the Army Air Corps in Detmold,

Germany and told him who I was, where I was from, and what I needed. I had to get one passenger from Deelen to RAF Gütersloh by mid-afternoon the following day, and I also required a low-loader vehicle to transport the unserviceable helicopter to Detmold for a replacement engine to be fitted. I was somewhat surprised when he didn't question me as I expected him to. Instead, he said "Ok, Mr Riley, need to know eh, don't worry, leave everything to me". The fact that he had said 'need to know' could only mean that he thought we were on some sort of, officially sanctioned, clandestine Special Forces mission, so I thought it might be prudent to leave him in his blissful state of ignorance.

The following morning a helicopter arrived to pick up 'Captain Mick' and he was safely dispatched, in good time for his appointment at RAF Gütersloh. At least the main objective of the sortie had been achieved. All I needed to do now was get back before ten-thirty on Wednesday morning and I would have nothing much to worry about. That didn't happen.

We low-loaded the stricken aircraft back to Detmold and a new engine was fitted and ready for flight testing on Tuesday. Everything was looking good until the new engine failed to meet the standards laid down in the Flight Test Procedure and a second engine had to be fitted.

We were eventually ready to head back to the UK, but by then it was Wednesday afternoon. In a phone-call back to base I had been told that my absence from the weekly prayers had been noted, not only by the adjutant but also by the C.O.

Meanwhile, there were rumblings in the corridors of power. The Foreign and Commonwealth Office made an enquiry to Group Headquarters in London asking why British soldiers, in civilian clothes, had flown into a foreign country without the mandatory diplomatic clearance. Group Headquarters, of course, had no idea what the fuck was going on. The commander of the Special Forces Group, Brigadier Peter de la Billiere, handed the enquiry down to the C.O. of 22 SAS, Colonel Mike Rose, to provide some answers.

The next morning, I was summoned to the adjutant's office and told to be prepared for an interview with the C.O. The adjutant, Captain Sam Mallard, was a regular squash partner of mine and a good friend, but today he had his serious head on. "Red. What the fuck have you been up to now?" he said. "On second thoughts don't bother telling me, you can save it for the boss. He's rather looking forward to seeing you."

41

Officers in the SAS are always referred to as 'boss'. Anyone other than a commissioned officer is referred to by their Christian or nickname.

The boss spoke. "Morning Red, no bullshit, just tell me what happened."

I told the boss the story just as I have told it to you.

"Do you have any regrets?" asked the C.O.

Thinking that I was about to get the sack, I gave him my reply. "I do regret putting you in an embarrassing position but, to be honest, if I thought I could get away with it I'd probably do the same again."

The boss looked thoughtfully at me and pushed the papers in front of him to one side. "You've just saved your skin Red by being truthful with me," he said. "Now fuck off out of my office and get on with your job, while I try and clear up the mess you've created."

"Thanks, boss," I said, as I left, giving Sam a big smile and a thumbs-up on the way out.

It would turn out to be far from the last time Mike Rose would save my skin.

Back at my desk, I pondered about just how fortunate I had been. I felt sure that any other C.O. would have had me sacked. I was determined that things were going to change and I made a promise to myself, right there and then, that from that moment on I would start to behave like a mature and well-disciplined warrant officer. Deep down inside me though, I had a nagging inkling that there was little or no chance that I would be able to keep that promise.

CHAPTER ELEVEN
OPERATION CORPORATE

When the regiment first moved into Bradbury Lines it had a large central Parade Ground. Not a facility that the SAS tended to make good use of, since marching about was not something they were likely to spend much of their time doing. In 1982 the Parade Ground was used to house a large marquee-like aircraft hangar and was laid out as a helicopter landing site, for use by day or night. It also had parking spaces for up to three helicopters.

It was a chilly spring morning and I had left my home at about six-thirty to give me time to run the five miles, or so, into work. By the time I had showered and had breakfast it was coming close to nine o'clock when I arrived at my office. There was a note on my desk, for my urgent attention, from Major Clive Fairbrother. The note explained that the queen's birthday was not too far away and the regiment would be holding a parade to commemorate the occasion. Since the regiment had not marched together for such a long time – a rather poor state of affairs in Clive's opinion – any members of the regiment not on essential operations would need to practise marching if they were to maintain the standards expected of one of the Army's finest infantry units. He pointed out that the parade ground was, at present, being inappropriately used and that rehearsal needed to get started as soon as possible. He also made it clear that not only was I required to move the hangar, but the whole square had to be cleared before the end of play that day. I was stunned. I just could not see how I would be able to dismantle the hangar and transfer it to another site in less than a day. There was also all the equipment and engineer's office from inside to consider, not to mention, of course, the helicopters.

I picked up the note and stormed across the square to Clive's office.

"Boss, this is outrageous. How can I possibly have this completed by the end of the day?" I said somewhat disrespectfully.

"What's the date on that note, Red?" asked Clive with a grin.

"First of April 1982 ... April first ...You bastard,' I said even more disrespectfully.

The rumour going around that day was that Argentinian forces were about to invade the Falkland Islands. The consensus was that this was, obviously, another April Fools' Day joke. More than likely started by members of the Intelligence Corps, and it was not a very good one at that.

It made no sense at all, to anyone, that the Argentinians would invade some little-known British Islands which everyone I spoke to assumed lay somewhere off the mainland of Scotland. This whole story just reinforced our opinion that the term Army Intelligence was, without a doubt, an oxymoron and the spoof was nowhere near as well thought out as Clive's.

About ten-thirty the following morning I received a call from Joyce in the telephone exchange next door to my office. She told me that all heads of departments were to attend prayers in the regimental briefing room immediately. Prayers on a Friday, especially at such short notice, were unheard of, so I guessed there must be something serious in the offing. As I entered the briefing room I realised that the rumours of an invasion had not been a substandard April Fools' day spoof after all. Spread across the wall were three large maps, the largest being a Transverse Mercator Projection of the world. The second was a standard Topographic Chart of South America from Buenos Aires in the north to Tierra del Fuego in the south. And finally, a one-to-a-half-million-scale map of the Falkland Islands, remarkably close to Antarctica.

The I.O, intelligence officer, Ron, opened the briefing and explained that, at that very moment, Argentinian marines were invading the British Sovereign Territory of the Falkland Islands almost eight thousand miles away in the South Atlantic Ocean. The director of Special Forces was at present, attending a meeting at the Cabinet Office Briefing Room, known to all as COBRA and chaired by the prime minister, Margaret Thatcher. The chief of the defence staff had already been instructed to prepare a counter-operation, including the assembly of a Task Force capable of sailing down to the South Atlantic to deal with the situation. All units likely to be involved in the Task Force were now to prepare for war. Twenty-Second Special Air Service Regiment was designated as one such unit. The counter operation was given the codename 'Operation Corporate'.

CHAPTER TWELVE

The following few days were hectic. We still had our anti-terrorist role to fulfil but requests for helicopter flying hours in support of Operation Corporate increased the workload of all the flight personnel dramatically. I found it easier to sleep on the floor of my office rather than driving home to Moreton each evening, as did some of the other guys. There was not one complaint from any member of the team even though they were having to work around the clock to meet the demand, grabbing meals and a few hours' sleep at irregular and intermittent intervals. There are normally, strictly enforced flying and duty time limits for pilots but, as Corporate began to gain momentum, these limits had to be overridden and I left it up to the individuals to let me know if they felt that they were no longer fit to fly.

The, newly appointed, regimental operations officer, Crocker, was required to attend numerous meetings in London as the Task Force was being prepared, but now the reason for our trips had taken on a new meaning and they were strictly for business. Once that business was done we would fly back to Hereford regardless of the weather, the time of day or our extramarital affairs.

On the night of the tenth of April at about ten-thirty, I lifted off from our group headquarters at the end of the Kings Road in London. I spoke to Barbara, who was the duty Air Traffic Controller at Battersea Heliport that night. She told me that there was a band of thunderstorms just west of the city and she strongly advised me to divert to the Heliport and stay overnight. As much as I appreciated the offer I felt duty bound to decline and decided that, in this instance, Corporate would have to take precedence over Copulate.

Flying through a band of active thunderstorms, at night, and with no weather radar is not something for the faint-hearted. We tightened our seatbelts as the cloud base lowered and the rain started, light at first, but quickly increasing until it was lashing against the windscreens, making the wipers totally ineffective. I lowered my helmet visor over my face, normally used to protect my eyes from the glare of the sun, but now it was needed to safeguard me from temporary blindness from the lightning flashes. As the turbulence increased from moderate to severe the rain simultaneously transformed into hail, crashing into the aircraft like a scatter gun. The maelstrom continued for about twenty minutes, but it seemed to me like an awful lot longer. Coming out of the cloud we began to make out the lights of Oxford and as things started to settle back down to normal Crocker was able to speak. "As soon as we get back I want you to go straight into quarantine, Red," he said. "You won't need any kit. Just make your way down to Pontrilas, without speaking to anyone, and stay there until further notice."

There was no point in me asking any questions since I knew he wouldn't be giving me any answers.

Quarantine is used to isolate an individual, as much as possible, to minimise the risk of a security leak prior to the start of an operation. No, contact with family or friends. No relaxing visits to the pub or popping into the local shop to pick up a daily newspaper and exchange a few pleasantries with the amiable storekeeper, who might be very interested in getting to know where Special Forces are being deployed to next. No telephone, no internet or access to a post box. Even the most trusted of individuals could, inadvertently, let slip information about any planned deployment. Possibly even by talking in their sleep or writing something down without it being intended to be read by anyone else.

It was close to midnight as we landed on the square in Hereford. Normally I would help the engineers to put the aircraft away for the rest of the night, but tonight things were different. Almost invariably, we would crack open a couple of cans of beer before sitting down for a brief chat about life in general and, of course, about how the helicopter was performing and whether any unscheduled maintenance needed to be done before being flown again. I would then sign the Flight Authorisation Sheet, which had to be done before leaving the office and the RAF Form 700, a military version of the civilian Flight Technical Log used for all aircraft throughout the Navy, Army, Royal Marines and the Royal Air Force.

But, tonight, none of the routine administration would be completed. Even though Crocker and I were good friends he was also my superior officer. He had given me a clear and unambiguous direct order, which I was, duty bound, to obey. I had been instructed to make my way to Pontrilas without speaking to anyone. The fact that I didn't ask any questions at the time of the order, made it clear that I understood what I was being told. So, that is exactly what I intended to do.

Pete, the engineer, approached us as we left the aircraft, with two, freshly opened cans of Budweiser and his usual cheery. "Evening Boss. Red. How's things?"

He had a face like a slapped arse when the boss abruptly replied, "No thanks, Pete" and strode off towards his office in Regimental Headquarters.

He seemed close to tears as I added insult to injury when I just looked at him and, instead of my normal friendly reply and joining him for a drink, said not a word and set off in the opposite direction to my car.

My lasting memory of Pete is of him standing in the light of the hangar with a can of beer in each hand. He reminded me, very much, of a meerkat on sentry duty, head going from side to side as he watched us disappear, wondering what the fuck was going on.

As I switched on the ignition to start my car, I realised that I was very low on fuel (nothing new there then, I hear you say). I felt that I now had a dilemma. I could, quite easily, leave my car where it was, walk across to the guardroom and get the duty driver to take me to Pontrilas. This option would, almost inevitably, mean me having to speak to someone and therefore disobey the direct order, not something that I wanted to do. I decided that the better option would be to risk the drive and if I ran out of fuel then I would have to accept a moonlight stroll. But what if I had to leave my car abandoned on the A465? Operation Corporate sounded to me like it could develop into a full-scale war. People get killed in wars, full-scale or not. If I didn't make it back then my car might never be found, and my long-suffering wife would miss out on the resale value of a recently re-sprayed, eight-year-old Ford Cortina with superb go-faster stripes which I had fitted not more than a month earlier. The fuel gauge was reading 'empty' as I left Bradbury Lines but, fortunately, it proved to be as unreliable as the rest of the Cortina and I made it safely to the main gate of the Pontrilas Army Training Area, which was then being used as a temporary Military Quarantine facility.

The Ministry of Defence police officer, normally referred to as 'Mod Plod', looked at me rather sheepishly, as he quickly pushed away his reading material and took a sip from his mug

"Warrant Officer Riley for quarantine," I said, rather awkwardly, not really sure as to whether or not I was now breaking my orders.

"Ok, let's have a look," he replied, as he carefully positioned the steaming cup between the 'Action in the event of Terrorist Attack' register and the *Playboy* magazine he had just been leafing through.

I stood at the guardroom hatch whilst the 'Mod Plod' reached over to his left and picked up a book which he opened and scrolled down the page with his finger. Looking up at me he asked me for my 'last three', which meant that he wanted me to recite the last three digits of my Army number. An Army number, then consisting of eight digits, was allocated uniquely to each individual serviceman, or woman, and would remain on record at the Ministry of Defence in perpetuity and is something that any service person will never forget.

'Nine six eight' I replied.

He nodded and then appeared to make a tick against, what I assumed to be, my name.

He was grossly overweight, sporting long unkempt sideburns and a thick moustache. He almost seemed to topple from his stool as he reached across to his right to pick up the phone.

"One for quarantine," he said abruptly, after a few seconds, before slamming the phone down.

"Wait there. Someone on their way to collect you," he almost shouted to me rather grumpily before closing the hatch in my face, almost as though he had been caught with his trousers around his ankles. To this day, I am convinced that he had been.

CHAPTER THIRTEEN

A few minutes later Lofty, who I knew to be the camp sergeant major, turned up looking like he had just been dragged out of bed. Which was hardly surprising since, by that time, it must have been well past one o'clock in the morning. The usual friendly dialogue and banter were left out that night and I followed Lofty, in silence, as he ambled towards one of the unlit barrack blocks. His gait seemed to be made more unusual by the fact that he had an almost permanent stoop, probably due to his stature of over six foot four inches.

My new accommodation was a small barrack room holding only eight old-fashioned, metal single beds, with a steel locker and bedside table for each bed space. At the far end of the room was a door displaying a sign 'Ablutions'.

There was no one else in the room so I assumed that I was either the first to arrive or the rest of the guys, preparing to go to war, were already bedded down in the adjacent barrack blocks.

"The mess hall is directly across the road. Breakfast six-thirty to eight," said Lofty, stifling a yawn.

"You'll find everything you need in your locker. Good night and god bless," he said leaving me to settle down for the night.

There was no sight or sound of any other person on camp as I walked across to the mess hall for breakfast the following morning. Expecting to find the place full of hungry squaddies, all stuffing their faces, before being sent off to the unfolding adventure close to the Antarctic, I was disappointed, instead, to find yet another empty room. Not even a cook or someone to keep the dining hall clean and tidy. The lights were on but the place was eerily quiet. On the serving counter, there was a solitary bain marie which felt warm. I lifted the lid and discovered a prepared and ready plated breakfast of eggs, bacon, sausage and beans which, assuming it was for me, I sat and ate at the nearest table which had been set for one.

For the next three days, I lived a bizarre existence not having contact with any other living soul. I spent the vast majority of my time sitting on my bed reading, and three times a day I wandered across to the empty mess, more out of boredom than hunger, to discover what culinary delights had been left for me to tuck into.

Not only was my solitary confinement becoming tedious, I was also beginning to get worried. Surely, by now, the task force had been assembled and a large number of the Regiment must, without a doubt, be part of it. Could it be possible that not only, had the task force been assembled but it was, at that very moment, sailing towards the Falkland Islands via Ascension? Could it also be possible that the bastards had left me behind?

I was eating my fourth, unbelievably dull, breakfast in 'Camp Solitude', as I had begun to call the place whenever I spoke to myself. And I didn't just talk to myself. I had full blown, two- way conversations with the mirror, my hand, the burnt sausage on my plate, in fact, anything that I thought would listen to me. As I was waiting for a reply from the sausage, the door of the mess hall swung open and in stooped Loftie. The sight of another human being brought tears of joy to my eyes and I became almost ecstatic when he actually spoke.

"Morning Red, how's the scran?" he asked with a cheery smile.

"Err... fine," I lied, as I coughed up a bean.

"Yeah, Andy, the chef sure does a mean breakfast. He only came on a six-month attachment from the catering corp twelve years ago, and we've refused to let him go back ever since," he said as he sat down beside me.

"Believe it or not, Andy was trained at the Savoy, or some posh gaff like that before he joined up. Bloody great cook and a hell of a nice guy."

My ears were ringing pleasantly at the sound of another person's voice. I couldn't comment on whether Andy was a nice guy, never having seen him. And I thought it better to keep my opinions on his cooking to myself.

"No doubt you'll be pleased to hear that, unlike our superb chef, we are letting you go," he added, almost melodically. "A car will be at the gate at nine. Good luck and stay safe my friend," he said as he shook my hand before turning to leave.

The car was already waiting for me when I got to the main gate a little before the arranged time. There was an envelope on the front passenger seat addressed 'Personal and private. W.O. Red Riley'.

"Morning mate," I said to the driver, who I didn't recognise.

"Good morning, sir," he replied.

"Hope you know where we are going cos I don't have a fucking clue," I mumbled, as I put the envelope on my knee and strapped myself in.

"Century House in London sir," came the reply in a more formal tone than I was used to.

I had never been to Century House but I knew, roughly, where it was. I felt sure that it was the headquarters of MI5, the UK security services. But it could have been MI6. I couldn't have cared less, and I had no idea what the difference was anyway. I was just glad to get away from Camp Solitude and Andy's cooking. It didn't surprise me one jot that he had been given the boot from the Savoy, or wherever it was, and ran away to join the Army – his food was absolutely crap.

CHAPTER FOURTEEN
OPERATION LOCAL

I sat back to enjoy the ride as we picked up the M55 motorway just north of Ross-on-Wye. Time to open the envelope. Inside I found my passport, five hundred pounds in cash and a business-class, one-way ticket to Rio de Janeiro.

I was met at the entrance to Century House by a tall guy in a grey suit who introduced himself as Jeremy, followed by a jumble of letters and numbers which made no sense to me at all. He handed me a visitors' pass, which I hung around my neck, and I then followed him through the security barrier. Jeremy led the way, his footsteps echoing, as we passed down a long corridor lined with impressive looking portraits and large wooden doors leading off from both sides. At the first open door, we entered, what could probably best be described as, a conference room. A large, highly polished, wooden table stood in the centre with a dozen, or so, chairs around it. At one end of the table, there was a screen and projector next to a large whiteboard on which was written 'Operation Local' and underlined twice. Sitting alone at the table was Brummie, who I recognised from Hereford. Brummie's long sideburns and droopy moustache exemplifying, a Mexican, as many people referred to members of the SAS in those days. Only his steely blue eyes suggested that, in fact, his ancestors originated from much further north than South America.

Jeremy and I joined Brummie at the table.

"Any idea what's happening mate?" I asked in a whisper.

"Looks like we're off to Copacabana Beach. Other than that, I don't have the foggiest," he whispered in reply.

A short, portly, middle-aged man with a bald head and ridiculously bushy eyebrows came into the room carrying a box file and a clipboard. He stood facing us and slowly placed the file and clipboard on the table in front of him. As he did so, his hands then withdrew into the sleeves of his jacket which were much too long, reminding me of a tortoise retreating into its shell. There was a pregnant pause as he reached into his top pocket and took out a pair of pince-nez which he carefully secured onto the end of his nose.

"Good afternoon gentlemen," he began in a deep monotone voice.

'I am H2SO4UK'. (That may not have been exactly what he said, but I do recall it sounded more like a chemical formula, for some kind of sulphuric acid, rather than it did for an appointment title).

The tortoise's head emerged from his right sleeve as he pointed, very deliberately, towards Brummie.

"Warrant Officer Stone, yes?' he said with a nod. The specs, rather amazingly, staying firmly in place.

And then it was my turn to be confronted by the reptile.

"And Warrant Officer Riley," he mumbled, seeming to throw his voice to the end of his arm like a well-practiced ventriloquist.

"Yes," was the only word I could summon. A voice inside my head was screaming at me, 'For Christ sake, put that fucking thing back inside its shell!'

"Operation Local," continued H2-something-or-other.

"You two gentlemen will be part of a four-man Special Forces team deploying into South America in direct support of Operation Corporate. All you need to know at this stage is that you are to move forward to Rio de Janeiro and await further instructions," he said slowly as he opened the lid of the box file.

"You have your civilianised documentation and airline tickets. Please leave your military ID cards and your dog tags on the table before you leave here today." He took out two large brown envelopes from the file.

"Mister Stone. In this there are five thousand Brazilian pesos and one thousand US dollars"' he said casually, sliding the package across the table.

"Mister Riley, your envelope contains the same, plus an extra twenty thousand US for you to lease an aircraft of some sort, if necessary." The much larger envelope being nudged towards me as he spoke.

We were given two telephone numbers and the name of a hotel. Jeremy explaining that the second phone number should only be used as a back-up. Our instructions were to travel together and, under no circumstances, were we to acknowledge anyone else if we happened to recognise them. Once ensconced into our hotel rooms one of us was to ring the number and ask for Mr Brooksbank, nothing more. We would then be told where and when to meet, for us to be given any further instructions.

"I believe you already have sufficient sterling to purchase whatever you may need for travelling. Do you have any questions?" H2 asked, as the tortoise did a neat little trick of flicking off the pince-nez specs and slipping them deftly back into his top pocket.

CHAPTER FIFTEEN

Later that day, as we sat eating a curry in the small Indian restaurant on Lower Sloane street, Brummie and I concocted what we would use as our reason for the visit to Rio. We decided that the two of us would pretend to be fairly rich individuals who thought it might be a good idea to sample the delights of South America. Not a particularly well thought out cover story. But it was simple and, I suspect that our powers of reasoning and rational thinking had been affected by the fact that we were on our second pint of Indian lager, having earlier spent three or four hours in the Rose and Crown pub across the road.

The next morning, we sat in the Business Class section of a British Airways 747 bound for Galeão International Airport, quaffing champagne and eating a selection of canapés. A mug of tea and a NAAFI 'growler' – what we normally called a steak pie – was much more in keeping with our style. But we were making every effort to play our parts, as international playboys, to the full. It felt to me like a very strange way to be going to war.

Once we had settled into the small hotel in the city's Botafogo region, we rang the number we had been given and asked for Mr Brooksbank, as instructed. After a couple of minutes, a man's voice, with a slight Scottish accent, came on the line.

"Hi. My name is Tim," he said, and then without waiting for a reply went on.

"I will leave something for you with your hotel reception within the next few days. No need to call again unless you have serious problems." The line went dead.

"Not very friendly," I chuntered. "Do you fancy a walk to the beach and a couple of beers?" I asked. I didn't need a reply. Brummie already had his rucksack, stuffed with money and his swimming kit, over his shoulder and he was heading for the door.

Not until the third day did we receive an envelope, which had been left with reception, addressed only to our room number. Inside was a handwritten note with the details of a hotel, two telephone numbers, the name Mr Summerson and two airline tickets to Santiago de Chile for the following day.

The short notice of the next leg of our journey left us with something of a dilemma. We had the biggest part of ten thousand Brazilian pesos left between us. We thought it best not to change it into US dollars since that might draw, unwanted, attention to us. The best solution we could come up with was to spend it, but we only had that evening in which to do it.

I asked the receptionist if he could order a taxi for us and recommend a nightclub.

"You want with boys or girls?" he asked.

He looked a little surprised, even shocked, when we both exclaimed.

"Girls. Of course!"

He mentioned a couple of nightclubs and then added one which he said was good but "very expensive".

"That sounds perfect," I said as I stuffed a wad of pesos into his top pocket.

The name of the nightclub eludes me, but I do remember the flashing lights, thumping music and the scantily clad girls, happily helping us to reach our goal of spending what was left of our local currency.

The journey from Rio to Santiago was much further than I expected, almost two thousand miles. The flight taking more than five hours, which gave us plenty of time to sleep off our hangovers from the night before. I must admit I was beginning to get used to travelling business class with civilian airlines. It was a far cry from our normal form of air transport which was in the back of a military C130 cargo plane, affectionately known as Fat Albert. We were usually strapped for hours into a less than comfortable canvas seat with the deafening roar of the four turboprop engines reverberating around the cavernous fuselage and only a bucket in the corner to use as a toilet.

We checked into a small hotel in the Les Condes area of the city, not far from the incongruously named Prince of Wales Country Club. As we unpacked our meagre possessions in our shared room, a note appeared from under the door.

'Hilton Bar, Avenado Vitacura. Tonight, seven thirty to meet a friend,' it read.

We left in good time to take a stroll towards the San Cristóbal Hill

Monument, having a ten-quid bet between each other as to who the huge statue overlooking the capital was supposed to be. Brummie chose Saint Christopher and I plumbed for Christ the Redeemer. It wasn't until I was at Brummie's funeral recently that I remembered that I had never coughed up what I owed him.

As we sat drinking our second glass of the local Chicca beer, the Commanding Officer Designate of 22 SAS Lieutenant Colonel Neville Howarth, came into the bar and joined us at our table.

"We don't know each other. I just heard you speaking English and joined you for a drink," he said without any of the normal friendly formalities. "I will get a message to you, at your hotel for the next meeting."

I had not, then, been given any kind of training in clandestine operations or instructions on how to conduct meetings with agents. I later learned that the prescribed protocol for any meetings is to always start with the two principles. One, immediately verify how anyone at the meeting knows each other and two, confirm details of the next rendezvous.

Neville briefly brought us up to date with the situation in the South Atlantic. The Task Force had recently come under very severe attack, mainly from the Argentine Airforce. More than a dozen ships had already been damaged. The most serious being HMS *Sheffield*, which was lost on the fourth of May, HMS *Ardent* on the twenty-second of May, and he had heard, just that morning, that HMS *Antelope* had also been sunk. In the opinion of the Defence Chiefs, the main threat was, considered to be, from the Exocet missiles delivered by the Super Étendard jets flying out of the Rio Grande airbase on Tierra del Fuego. He made it abundantly clear that, unless something was done to curtail the success of the Argentinian Airforce, then the war was likely to be lost, in a very short time, and at a cost, possibly, of thousands of British lives.

"We will meet again tomorrow at about the same time. I will let you know where," Neville said sternly. "In the meantime Red, I want you to look at the possibility of getting an aircraft to get us to Punta Arenas, lease it, borrow it, steal it. Just do whatever it takes."

Before leaving he slid an envelope across the table containing a few hundred thousand Chilean pesos.

Early the next morning I turned up at the flying club at Tobalada Airfield with my mind firmly set on getting my hands on an aeroplane capable of getting us down to the area of the, precariously balanced, war.

I met a pilot, calling himself Jose, who operated a Beechcraft King Air, a twin-engine light aircraft, usually configured to seat about eight passengers and with, just about, sufficient range to get us the twelve hundred nautical miles or so I was looking for. I showed the operator my British Airline Transport Pilots Licence and told him that I needed to get a BBC crew down to Punta Arenas. He agreed to lease me the King Air provided he could fly with me to bring it straight back. The hourly rate was three hundred US dollars and the round trip was likely to take somewhere in the region of about twelve flying hours. A bargain, I thought, at less than four thousand dollars. Somewhat less of a bargain, however, when he added that I would also have to leave a deposit of fifteen thousand dollars, again in cash, before taking off from Santiago. I was in no mood for bargaining. I agreed on the deal and told him that I would call him the following day to confirm the number of passengers and what time we would like to leave.

CHAPTER SIXTEEN

That evening we again met Neville, and again he was alone. We had still not set eyes on the missing, fourth member, of the team. He went through the, now familiar, agent meeting procedure, and then went on to tell us that a political decision had been made by the Chilean Government. British troops would not be allowed on the neutral territory of Chile whilst a state of war existed between them and Argentina and we were about to be interned. This meant that we should expect to spend the duration of the war in prison, in order to avoid the government any embarrassment. There was no way any of us wanted, or intended to, allow this to happen, so we hastily, put together a plan. It was agreed that we would not return to our hotel rooms that evening. We would, instead, stay out for the night and meet up at Tobalada Airfield as soon as the gates opened the following morning, and get away from Santiago as quickly as possible. Fortunately, Jose, who I had agreed to do the lease deal with, was one of the first to arrive and didn't seem to be the least bit surprised to find us waiting for him. Unfortunately, Neville and the fourth team member where nowhere to be seen and we had, of course, no way of contacting them.

I introduced Brummie as a part of the BBC television crew, mumbling something about a camera grip gaffer, or some such nonsense, and explained that the rest of the team were on their way. Handing over the brown envelope, containing the twenty thousand dollars, which I had been given before leaving London, I asked if we could get ready to depart as soon as possible. We had no way of knowing if the other half of the team were already languishing in a Chilean prison so we decided that we would leave as soon as we were ready, regardless of whether they turned up or not. As Jose, or whatever his real name was, sat diligently counting out the money, a taxi pulled up at the door. Out jumped Neville and someone that we both, instantly, recognised – Bernie Lane. None of us needed any introduction, Bernie and Brummie had spent many years together in the SAS and I had known him for the past three years or so. I introduced Neville and Bernie as the last two members of the BBC crew, deciding this time to play it safe and leave out their job titles. Jose seemed to be completely unfazed by the fact that we had no baggage between us and just nodded when I asked if we could get on our way as soon as possible since the gaffer would like to get to Tierra del Fuego before last light if possible.

As my co-pilot filed the flight plan, I cast my eyes over the en route weather forecast, paying little attention to it, to be honest, since I intended to get away from Santiago regardless of what the elements had to throw at us. Quite a lot as it turned out.

There was a fairly strong wind blowing directly across the north–south aligned runway, over three thousand feet in length, so I elected to take off on runway One Nine in order to save me a one hundred and eighty-degree turn, before heading south towards the Antarctic. For more than a thousand miles the navigation could barely be easier. All I had to do was keep the Pacific Ocean on my right and the towering Andes mountain range on my left and we would be almost certain to stay clear of Argentinian airspace. But what benefits the mountains gave by guiding us safely to Punta Arenas they took away from us in the form of turbulence.

Turbulence so extreme that our little turboprop aircraft was in danger of being torn asunder.

When the wind hits the side of a mountain range – and the Andes is the longest mountain range in the world – severe, orographic, or mountain wave turbulence, can occur. Powerful up-draughts, known as anabatic winds, and down-draughts, known as katabatic winds cause enormous disturbances to the air, sometimes as far away as one hundred miles in the lee of the range. Throughout, just about, the whole of our journey, the turbulence was, what can only be described as, very severe. It was very distressing for everyone on board, including me, although the co-pilot seemed to be remarkably relaxed. I was acutely aware that structural damage could result and that light aircraft, such as the one we were in, had been known to have their wings ripped off, resulting in predictable consequences. All on board were hugely relieved when we landed safely at Punta Arenas, the most southerly airfield on the South American mainland and a short hop from Tierra del Fuego.

We were met at the bottom of the aircraft steps by a small, Latin American-looking guy, in a grey suit and brightly coloured tie. He shook hands with Neville, the obvious leader of our small team, who I guess must have displayed the airs of a lieutenant colonel, whilst the rest of us were mere warrant officers. Without introducing himself to anyone other than our leader, he led us across the dispersal area and into the small terminal building. After negotiating a series of corridors, we were escorted straight into the back of a waiting minibus with blacked-out windows, having circumnavigated any of the normal arrival procedures.

It was not until many years after the war, when I returned to Santiago, that I learned that Jose the Pilot had, shortly after our trip, been killed whilst flying his small turboprop aircraft. I have always suspected that he had been employed by the Chilean Intelligence Service, but any assistance we might have been given by the government had to be completely deniable and provided to us as covertly as possible.

We were driven through the town of Punta Arenas to a small port and then onto a ferry which took us across the Strait of Magellan to, an even smaller port, of Porvenir. Eventually, we arrived at an isolated farmhouse, where we were left and told to make ourselves comfortable for the night. The farmhouse was enclosed by a high fence and heavy wooden gates. There were several outbuildings, one of which housed the hefty, diesel-fuelled, generator, the only source of electricity for the house. It had quite a few bedrooms, all of them comfortably furnished with clean bedding and fresh towels. The kitchen was stocked with enough tinned food to keep the four of us going for months. There was a large cellar which was packed with more quasi-military equipment than you would be likely to find in your average quartermaster's store. The kit ranged from clothing and sleeping bags to survival rations, cooking stoves and mountaineering equipment. There was even a RIB, rigid inflatable boat, with an outboard motor, and two cross-country motorbikes. In a small room, off the main hallway, was a satellite telephone system, already set up and working, and capable of providing secure communications back to our base in Hereford.

Although we now had enough equipment to survive the harsh winter conditions and operate across the rugged terrain of Tierra del Fuego, we were still more than one hundred miles from our target, the Airforce Base at Rio Grande. A long way if we had to make it by foot. Even if we drove to the Argentine border we would still be left with a walk of thirty or forty miles over very inhospitable terrain, all of it in enemy occupied territory. We all agreed that our best option would be to get our hands on a helicopter. But we had little doubt that the chances of that happening were extremely remote.

CHAPTER SEVENTEEN

Our heads were buzzing as we settled down for the night, thinking how, just the four of us, could possibly inflict any damage on the enemy, let alone enough to make an impact on the war. We had to try to minimise or, better still, stop altogether, the Super Étendards and their lethal Exocet missiles from destroying any more of the Task Force ships before it was too late.

I have no idea how Neville was able to arrange it, but the next morning we managed to get on to the local Defence Force Base, which was equipped with a selection of fixed-wing aircraft and helicopters, most of them being of American design. Not only that, but we also finished up in the office of the base commander, who was very friendly and spoke English with, what I can best describe as a rather educated Oxbridge accent. He made it abundantly clear to us that he had complete authority in this part of the world and that talks of internment, or just about anything else, from bureaucrats in Santiago were of no consequence to him.

Neville told the commander that I was a pilot and asked if it was possible to lease a helicopter from a civilian company on the island.

"It is not possible to lease a helicopter from anywhere on Tierra del Fuego," said the Commander thoughtfully. "However, I may be able to help," he added as he looked across at me.

"Mister Riley, please go with my Head of Training and show him that you can fly. In the meantime, I would like to chat, over a cup of coffee, to Colonel Neville about my time at your wonderful Royal Military Academy Sandhurst and the nightlife of Camberley."

The helicopter was a 'Huey', which was, and still is, the nickname for the UH1, American Utility Helicopter. Then the most ubiquitous and prolific helicopter in the world. It became famous in the sixties when thousands were built and used in the Vietnam war. The Huey was a remarkably simple aircraft to fly and I had no trouble impressing the instructor with my inherent flying ability.

Back at the office, there was, almost, a party atmosphere with the commander laughing and reminiscing about all the great times he had as a young officer in the UK, when The Beatles, mini-skirts and free love were all the rage.

He poured us all a small glass of some local grog and stood to attention behind his desk to propose a toast.

"Gentlemen... comrades," he said, raising his glass. "To Her Majesty the Queen and the success of your mission."

"The Queen," we all harmonised, knocking back the grog.

"Mister Riley. We are very happy with your flying, but you need to consolidate your training. You may use the helicopter to improve your skill and, of course, that is best done flying solo," continued the commander. "You may also take your friends along with you for the ride, but you must not, under any circumstances, fly into Argentinian airspace." "Well of course not, sir," I lied. "And thank you."

Flying around in circles for me to improve my flying skills on the Huey was not an option. We felt that we had to do something and do it without wasting any more time, and that would mean not only flying into Argentinian airspace, but we would also have to get as close as possible to the enemy airfield. Crossing into enemy territory from a neutral country in a stolen helicopter was going to be fraught with danger. Getting to within a mile, or so, of the Rio Grande Airbase, with its low-level air defence systems and airfield perimeter protection forces was going to be perilous in the extreme.

It was decided that only Brummie would fly with me, armed with nothing more than an SLR, – a single lens reflex camera. That way if, or, possibly more likely, when, we were shot down, at least only half of the team would have been lost.

We sat down together studying the maps and considering what we were aiming to achieve. We had both been in the Army long enough to know that before undertaking any action it is essential to define an aim which should always be clear and unambiguous. Our aim was to take aerial photographs of the airfield and aircraft dispersal areas at the Rio Grande Airforce Base and return with them to our Forward Operating Base on Tierra del Fuego. Apart from the main aim, we felt that there was a reasonable chance that we may pick up some bonuses along the way. We could possibly find out at what range the low-level air defence system would become effective and, as we got closer, we might discover when the small arms fire of the perimeter protection forces came into play. Perhaps needless to say, but we were not looking forward to either of these bonuses. There was no doubt in our minds that this was going to be a very high-risk undertaking but we took a minute to consider the positives. There was a chance that we might not get picked up on radar or be seen by anyone on the ground. There was also the possibility that, even if we did get seen, then we could be mistaken for Argentinian Airforce, since they also flew Hueys and it seemed likely that they were not an uncommon sight in that part of the world.

We were both fully aware that the odds were stacked against us, but the stakes were so high that we felt that we were left with no other alternative. The risks had to be taken.

My operational tours in Northern Ireland had taught me how best to avoid small arms fire from the ground. Fly ultra-low-level, as fast as possible, and follow an unpredictable track. We packed a small rucksack each with a basic survival kit in case we had to abandon the aircraft and tab it for thirty or forty miles back to the safety of the border. A walk across the country is referred to as a 'tab' in the Army, a 'yomp' in the Royal Marines and, I'm not sure, but possibly, a 'sashay' in the Royal Airforce.

I explained to Brummie the risks we were about to face and how the level of danger was likely to increase as we got closer to the target.

"Is there anything I should do if we do get hit?" asked Brummie with a worried look on his face.

"Oh yes," I replied. "There is a standard emergency procedure which you need to carry out, which I happen to have written down here," I said looking through my imaginary notes as if I wanted to make sure that he knew the procedure exactly.

"Yes, here it is," I recited, pretending to read it to him verbatim. "In the event of being struck by enemy fire the co-pilot should: One – immediately release his shoulder straps. Two – place both hands behind his neck. Three – bend his head between his knees and kiss his arse goodbye."

CHAPTER EIGHTEEN

On the evening of the twenty-first of May we were told that an eight man SAS patrol was lost somewhere on the island of Tierra del Fuego, and that Brummie and I should use the Chilean Airforce helicopter to help in the search for them. We were also warned that the area was likely to be teeming with enemy troops. We had no idea at the time what the patrol had been up to, but it later transpired, that they were part of Operation Plum Duff and had been tasked to carry out a reconnaissance of the airbase at Rio Grande which B Squadron, led by their newly appointed Commander were planning to attack within the next few days. We both reckoned that searching for the patrol would be futile, especially if they were in Argentina. As soon as the experienced troopers heard the very recognisable thwack of the Huey rotor blades they would, almost certainly, assume that we were the enemy and immediately go to ground and we would be likely to see nothing. If we did happen to spot them and subsequently fly towards them they would almost certainly consider us to be the enemy and try to shoot us down. We would, of course, bear the lost patrol in mind as we overflew the area, but we would, primarily, be concentrating on our real aim of getting as close to the airfield as possible and taking a few snaps of the place.

The weather forecast was not good, low cloud and freezing rain showers across the whole of our planned route. Freezing rain is extremely dangerous for a helicopter, so not only would we be trying to avoid the anti-aircraft defences and the snow-capped hills, but we would also need to dodge around any showers we might encounter.

Shortly after take-off, we descended to ultra-low level, generally flying in the valleys, well below the tops of the hilly terrain, but never more than fifty feet above the surface to keep below the defensive radar coverage. As we crossed into enemy territory navigation became extremely difficult. Rather than simply maintaining a steady heading, as we normally would, we constantly steered off course to the left or right, sometimes by as much as sixty degrees, to tack towards our target like a yacht approaching a harbour into a headwind. But Brummie's map reading proved to be outstanding and I could concentrate on looking ahead for perilous obstacles or wires strung across the valleys. If at any stage, we became uncertain of our position then our plan was to head south until we picked up the river and re-orientate ourselves.

"Ok, mate," I said as we got to within about ten miles of our goal. "Get ready to kiss your arse goodbye, we need to pop up to take a look."

I pulled back on the cyclic control and climbed quickly above the surrounding hills. We both scanned the horizon towards the east but the poor visibility revealed nothing but grey. Less than three seconds later we had dived back down into the relative safety of the valley. The poor visibility proved to be a double-edged sword, giving us some protection from being spotted by the mark-one eyeball on the ground, but also meaning that we would have to push our luck and get a lot closer before we would be able to see the airfield, and get pictures that would be of any use whatsoever. The only way we could hope to avoid being shot out of the sky was to pop up for very short periods of time in unpredictable locations and keep the number of times we exposed ourselves to an absolute minimum. At a range of fewer than two miles, we found ourselves in a valley running north to south with the airbase due east of use. A blast of arctic air surged into the cockpit as Brummie opened his side window ready to start shooting. Heading south, with the collective lever in my left hand, pulled up to maximum to gain as much speed as possible, I climbed up and out of the valley. There it was. The Rio Grande Airbase. It had to be the briefest of glimpses. Holding my breath in anticipation of the clatter of small arms fire smashing into the soft skin of the aircraft I rammed the cyclic control forward and dived at high speed back behind cover.

"Never felt a thing. Let's have another go," I shouted as we popped up for another three-second exposure. And again, we got down unscathed.

"Once more for luck," I – just about – heard Brummie shout over the sound of the wind rushing across his microphone.

"There you go, mate. That's your lot," I said, diving back into the valley. "Now shut that fucking window before we freeze to death, and let's get the hell out of here."

As I saw the river valley ahead of us I did a steep turn to the right, staying low and fast we headed generally west and back towards safety. Interestingly we spotted not one of the enemy troops that were said to be 'teeming across the area'.

We eventually met up with the lost patrol and I was given the job of getting their weapons back to the UK. I was issued with the documentation appointing me as a 'Queen's Messenger' thereby allowing me to carry anything in the form of diplomatic baggage throughout my journey without it leaving my sight. Diplomatic bags are free from any scrutiny by customs officers or any other officials. I was booked into the first-class cabin of the British Caledonian flight from Santiago to London and allocated not one, not two, but three seats. The two spare seats were needed for the very large black bags that were not allowed to leave my side. The large black bags containing a small arsenal of specialist weaponry.

After landing I was instructed to remain in my seat until all the other passengers had disembarked. Two bodyguard-like characters came on board to meet me and staggered under the weight of my baggage as they carried it down the aircraft steps and into the waiting vehicle. I was then driven, without any entry formalities, straight out of the airport and into our Group Headquarters on the Kings Road in Chelsea.

As I was unloading the bags and laying the weapons neatly out onto a table, Trevor Harley, a captain from 22 SAS in Hereford, came into the room.

"Hi, Red. Nice to see you, but what the hell are you doing here?" he asked.

"I just brought these weapons back from down south," I replied.

"You should never have been given that job. Anyone could have done it," he continued angrily. "Stay where you are till I sort this out."

He certainly didn't seem to be at all happy as he went out of the room and left me unpacking. I was also left wondering whether I was soon to be on my way home, or back to the airport, with another eight-thousand-mile journey ahead of me.

The airport it was. Trevor, not normally a grumpy sort, had stuffed a ticket, a few hundred dollars and the name of a hotel in Santiago into my hand and told me to get my arse back there as quickly as possible. As a soldier, mine was not to reason why. Mine was just to do or die. And so, I set off back to the war zone.

I was too late for that day's flight but the following morning I was once more, strapping myself into the, now familiar, first-class cabin.

"Hello, again Mister Riley. What a nice surprise," said the stewardess cheerily, as she handed me a glass of champagne. "You going back already? I must say, you don't look at all like the normal Queen's Messengers we have flying with us."

"No. Well... I'm just new to the job," I mumbled as I picked up the in-flight magazine with the clear intention of showing her that the conversation was over.

As soon as I got through passport control I made straight for the big yellow 'M' for MacDonald's. I was starving, having spent the complete flight pretending to be asleep to avoid any further chat with the inquisitive air hostess.

I spent the next few days in the Hilton Garden Inn, close to the airport.

The fourteenth of June was my birthday and I had just finished celebrating it, by sitting at the hotel bar on my own, when the barman came in from the back room clapping his hands.

"*Malvinas guerra terminado,*" or words to that effect, he said with a beaming smile on his face.

I looked at him with a gormless expression and a forced smile. Then, after thinking for a few seconds, he did his best to make me understand.

"Fucklands combat finish," he said thoughtfully.

"*Si, si comprende,*" I replied. "Fucklands war is over."

I laughed as I went to bed.

A day, or so, later I returned to Hereford after being debriefed in London. I never did find out why I had been sent back to Chile by Mister Grumpy, but for me, and everyone else I suppose, the Fucklands war was definitely over.

CHAPTER NINETEEN

In those days, the standard 'tour of duty', in other words, the length of time one could expect to remain in a particular job, was three years. My time as the SAS Flight Commander was, very sadly, about to come to an end. I certainly didn't relish the thought of going back to an appointment away from the Special Forces. Or, even worse, getting involved in training or instruction. But I had little choice. By that time, I had completed seventeen of the twenty-two years I needed to serve to qualify for a full Army pension.

The newly installed fax machine pinged and spewed out a form entitled 'Preference of Posting' with a note attached asking me to complete it and fax it back. I completed the form and made it clear that the preference for my next posting should be easy to satisfy. I asked to be sent to anywhere in the world other than Detmold in Germany. That done I stuffed the form back into the new-fangled machine and whisked it back to the Ministry of Defence in London, expecting to be informed of where my future would lie within a month or two.

I was surprised to say the least, when, the following day, I received notice that, not only was I posted to Detmold, but I was posted almost immediately and should expect to end my career there!

The department at the MOD which then dealt with postings and promotions within the Army Air Corps was known as AG-14, which was run by a colonel with the support of a warrant officer acting as his chief clerk.

Thinking that I had been the subject of a joke set up by the warrant officer, who I remembered vaguely from my days at Middle Wallop, I was straight on the phone to AG-14. I asked the chief clerk to confirm that he had issued the posting order as a prank emphasised by the fact that it had been promulgated so quickly. His attitude was particularly unfriendly and I was taken aback when he reasserted that the order was absolutely correct. He tried to convince me that, with new technology (by which I presume he meant the, recently introduced, fax machine), rapid responses were set to become the norm, and that the colonel and himself were simply being efficient and therefore there was nothing more to discuss.

"Wait a minute," I said, "that's a load of old bollocks. I demand to have a personal interview with the Colonel and since he is so fucking efficient, let's make it tomorrow morning".

There was a rather long silence broken only by some distant voices and then the sound of footsteps returning to the phone.

"The colonel will see you tomorrow at eleven hundred hours," said the Chief Sodding Clerk. "Do not be late."

'Oh, I won't be late. You can rest assured' I said. And slammed the phone down.

Early the next morning I jumped into a 'cab', as helicopters are, invariably, referred to in the Army Air Corps, and flew myself down to Battersea Heliport.

Barbara seemed to be most impressed when I turned up be-suited, rather than wearing my normal jeans, desert boots and a tatty old denim shirt with holes in it.

After a brief peck on the cheek I was off in a different kind of 'cab' – this one was a London taxi and I was on my way around to my appointment with the eminent 'Oberst Fuhrer', in charge of posting and promotions.

I arrived at the sour-faced chief clerk's office a good ten minutes before my appointment time and sat in silence as I waited to be summoned. Normally, if two soldiers of similar rank were sat in the same room for more than a minute or two, a good old chat would ensue, but today there was nothing but silence and tranquillity in the air.

On the stroke of eleven, I made a very deliberate and obvious glance at my G10 watch. A G10 watch was a basic and standard timepiece issued to most soldiers from, what was known as, the G10 store. As a pilot, I was, of course, entitled to be issued with the far more prestigious 'Air Crew Chronometer', but the extra dials, knobs and sweep hands just did nothing for me so I preferred to stick with something that would simply tell me the time.

The silence continued. The minutes ticked away and the 'Fuhrer's' door remained closed.

At exactly fifteen minutes past eleven, I jumped to my feet, picked up my bag and declared. "Right, I'm off."

The chief clerk looked at me in astonishment and blustered, "You can't just leave. The colonel is expecting to see you."

"Just watch me mate. You can tell him that I expect to be treated with some respect. He didn't even have the decency to apologise for keeping me waiting, so you can also tell him to stick his posting up his arse," I said as I slammed the door behind me.

Flying back towards Hereford I had time to ponder the consequences of my actions in the corridors of power in Whitehall. It was a pretty safe bet that by the time I got back, the Fuhrer and his untermensch would be compiling a list of charges, no doubt, including insubordination towards a senior officer. A charge which was, considered to be, a serious offence throughout the Armed Forces at that time.

As a highly qualified pilot, I felt confident that I would have little difficulty in finding a well-paid flying job in 'civvy street' and I therefore decided, I wasn't going to go to Detmold and that my best option would be to leave the Army as soon as possible. Leaving before completing my contracted period of twenty-two years would mean that I would have to forego any pension, but I was determined and willing to accept the fact.

I did feel very sad. The Army had been my life since I was seventeen and, since the age of fifteen, it had really been the only thing I had ever wanted to do. As a civilian, I would probably have to accept a job flying back and forth to the North Sea oil rigs based in Aberdeen, in the far north of Scotland. It would mean leaving our family home in Hereford and taking our three children out of the schools they were now happily ensconced in. But I felt strongly that I was being unfairly treated by the Army Air Corps and I was unwilling to acquiesce to their demands simply to retain my pension, which I would qualify for after another three years' service.

As I closed down the engine on the square in Sterling Lines I was met by Pete Guthrey, one of the flight 'Blackies'. The word 'Blackie', incidentally, is not intended to be racist, in any way. It is merely a traditional term used to describe an Aircraft Engineer specialising in airframes and engines. A 'Greenie', on the other hand, is an engineer specialising in Aircraft Avionics.

Pete the 'Blackie' strode towards me with an oily rag in one hand and an enormous spanner in the other. "Sounds like you're in the shit again, mate," he said with a smile. "Bob Noxious wants to see you in his office straight away."

We didn't call the new adjutant 'Bob Noxious' for nothing. Bob sat behind his desk with his face looking like a slapped arse, just as it always did. He had a notoriously abrasive manner and rarely cracked a smile. But he had a wicked sense of humour which appealed to me enormously. I liked and respected him very much – still do, come to think of it. "What the fuck have you been up to now?" he hissed. "Some irate colonel from the M.O.D. has been having a right go at the boss about you. Reckons you should be thrown in jail and left to rot for the way you gobbed off at him and his mate. And then you had the cheek to leave the poor sod with no one to talk to."

I explained what had happened, admitting that I, probably had, been insubordinate. Looking back, I suppose I must have become used to being respected as an equal by everyone in the Special Forces Group, regardless of rank. Being considered to be an underling, who should do no more than obey orders, rubbed against the grain with me, and I felt I was unwilling to be treated that way.

The adjutant didn't smile – at least not externally. But I knew he sympathised with me, and I got the feeling that he would have reacted in pretty much the same way as I had.

"Wait there, Red," said Bob as he disappeared into the office next door.

A few minutes later the door opened and I was invited in to talk with the C.O.

The boss was the first to speak. "Well, Red, Bob has explained the reasoning behind your reputed insubordination and I think we should just put that behind us. You are obviously not happy with your future prospects in the Army Air Corps, so we have a proposal for you." He glanced across at the straight-faced Bob. "Why don't you come and join us?"

'Come and join you? If you mean transfer to the regiment Boss, can I remind you that I am thirty-six years old – the selection course would probably kill me," I replied.

"We are fairly sure you will survive despite your advancing years. Just let Bob know if you decide to give it a go, and he will get you on the next course starting in January. Let's face it your prospects are not looking too good at the moment, so you may as well give it your best shot," said the C.O. As he closed his diary, as if to indicate that the interview was over.

CHAPTER TWENTY
SAS SELECTION

There were over a hundred of us, SAS wannabes, lined up in three ranks outside Training Wing offices at six-thirty on a cold morning in January. We had been told to turn up on this, the first day of the selection course, dressed in 'clean fatigues' and PT vest, ready for a short warm-up run before breakfast. 'Clean fatigues' is a form of dress in the Army, best described as 'normal' working dress, which would consist of boots, trousers and a red or white, army issue, T-shirt.

Major Paddy Baxter was the Officer Commanding Training Wing, the department responsible for running the Regiment's, twice yearly, selection courses. Most courses started with around a hundred candidates and were expected to produce about ten 'badged' soldiers at the end of the course.

The O.C. training wing stood before us looking a little perplexed. He kept checking his watch and looking around as if he were waiting for someone, while we stood there gradually freezing our nuts off.

'I'm sorry guys, but the instructors who were going to take you for a little warm-up seem to have been delayed,' said Paddy in his soft Irish brogue. 'If they don't turn up in the next ten minutes or so we will cancel, and you can all shoot off for a nice warm shower and breakfast.'

I, and probably most of the other guys, couldn't help thinking, 'No fucking instructors! What a result – looks like this course is going to be an absolute doddle.'

Just then an old bloke, probably in his fifties, came around the corner, dressed in a scruffy coat, big scarf and a furry cap pulled down over his ears. He was pushing a wheelbarrow containing a bass broom, a rake and other cleaning paraphernalia.

Major Baxter stopped the old gent and had a couple of minutes' chat with him out of earshot from the squad. Paddy then turned towards us with a smile on his face. "This is Yorkie who works here keeping the place clean and tidy and, in the absence of the instructors, has very kindly agreed to take you for a short run. Just keep up with him please and, when he stops, break off for breakfast. I will see you later in the day."

There was a positive murmuring in the ranks. "This is going to be an absolute breeze keeping up with this old fogey who sweeps the camp. He'll probably be knackered after about ten minutes – happy days!"

There were lots and lots of cheerful smiling faces as we set off at a steady pace to follow 'Old Yorkie'.

An hour later there was not a smile to be seen. The old bastard just went on and on.

There then appeared physical training instructors (PTIs) along the route hurling abuse at those of us who were struggling to keep up. "Come on, you fucking idle wimps – if you can't keep up with the camp caretaker, how the fuck are you going to keep up with real soldiers?"

The insults spurred me on. I had to dig deep. I had to push myself as hard as I could. If I was going to get binned on the first day, then at least I would be able to say that I couldn't possibly have gone any faster, or any further.

Gradually, I started to move further up the field of runners. My legs felt like they were made of lead and my chest felt as it were about to explode. I just had to get past the candidate in front of me. And then another.

Suddenly, I could see Yorkie the caretaker, casually chatting away and rolling a cigarette. He was standing next to a four-ton truck and as I got alongside him I collapsed in a heap gasping for breath. Just then one of the instructors chirped up. "Right, you lot onto the trucks with Yorkie. The rest of the lazy twats can walk back to camp and pack their bags."

On the first day of the notorious SAS selection course, we had lost more than twenty aspiring SAS Troopers before breakfast.

By the end of the second week we were down to, I guessed, less than fifty. I couldn't be arsed counting how many of us were still in contention. I didn't care. But I knew that there were now only two trucks needed to cart us off to the Brecon Beacons, or some other gruesome countryside, every morning. Once there, we would spend hour after hour battling with tortuous terrain and weather just to get from one checkpoint to another.

The single thing I concentrated on was getting through one day at a time. The only way I could avoid being thrown off the course was to get around each route as quickly as I could, without hurting myself so badly, that I would be forced to withdraw due to injury.

Each day started at some ridiculously early hour. At the end of each day's torture, we were told only what time we should be ready to go and how much our Bergens should weigh. The weight had by then increased from thirty-five pounds to forty-five. We also had to carry a rifle and whatever water we thought we would need to last us through the day. The four-ton trucks would be parked up outside training wing, engines running and tailgates down. As each name was called, that person would step forward and have the weight of his rucksack checked by one of the directing staff, known to everyone as the D.S.

Immediately after climbing into the back of one of the trucks I would, invariably, dive straight into my doss-bag and get as much rest as possible. Although I suppose I must have done, I don't recall ever speaking to anyone else on the course. I needed to be single-minded, and I concentrated totally on getting from one checkpoint to another, in as short a time as possible, and getting through each day of selection.

It was early morning and pitch black when the truck pulled up, some-where in the remote countryside of Wales. The tailgate crashed down and I waited for my name to be called. There was, normally, a gap of five min-utes or so, between each candidate being sent on his way. When I lowered myself out of the truck I looked around in the darkness and the mist, hoping to get some clue as to where we might be. But all I could make out were the vague outlines of hills in every direction – fucking ugly black hills, which I couldn't even see the tops of.

I limped towards the D.S., map in hand, ready to receive details of my first checkpoint. By now my feet were in a pretty bad state. Both my big toenails were black and painful to touch. My heels and soles were covered in blisters, and getting my boots on and off at the start and end of each day, was a huge struggle, due to the amount of swelling.

The D.S. were not given to wasting words. Not once did I ever hear from them any expressions of encouragement or questions concerning my wel-fare. "You are here" they would say, pointing to an eight-figure grid refer-ence, "and your next checkpoint is..." Nothing more was ever said by any of the 'badged' soldiers who manned any of the checkpoints apart from the occasional "let me weigh your Bergen".

Once I got myself going the pain in my feet would begin to subside but the extra weight I was having to carry was beginning to take its toll. The shoulder straps were starting to cut into my upper trapezius muscles (not that I had that much to cut into, mind you), and the constant movement of the dead weight was rubbing into the flesh at the base of my spine.

I managed to get through another day, but I found it to be very tough. Back in my basha, as I struggled to get my boots off without removing too much skin, I decided that the time had come to take stock of my situation.

Test week was due to start after the following weekend. The weight we would be required to carry would soon increase to fifty pounds plus rifle and water. About seventy pounds in all. I was in poor physical shape and I had no doubt that the extra weight was going to be a big problem for me.

I sat on my bed and looked at my feet. Those feet of which of which I had always been so proud. Hitherto such things of beauty and, without a doubt, my most redeeming feature were now reduced to a hideous mess. Tears welled in my eyes as I remembered how, ever since basic training all those years ago, I had lovingly tended to my most precious assets. In recent times, I had been known (albeit in limited circles) as 'the best feet in the street'. And now here I was barely able to look at them without wanting to gag.

Perhaps it was time to throw in the towel. Everyone would understand, after all I was in my dotage by military standards, so I had a readily available excuse. And I was in the fortunate position of having the option to leave the Army and get a cushy, well-paid job in civvy street.

The routine for 'jacking', voluntarily withdrawing from the course, was simple – just stay in bed at the start of the day instead of lining up ready for another spell of agony. The idea certainly had a great deal of appeal to me, so my mind was made up. Fuck selection. I am definitely, going to jack it in. Tomorrow I will have a lie in, take a nice warm shower and, after a leisurely breakfast, make my way over to the office to be formally sent back to the Army Air Corps – I couldn't think of anything better, I had no doubt whatsoever. I was looking forward to the next day, and there was no way that I was going to change my mind.

CHAPTER TWENTY-ONE

During the night, I had a change of heart. I decided that I would stick with the course, but it might be necessary for me to resort to a modicum of cheating, in order to increase the chances of me completing it from – 'no fucking chance whatsoever', to – 'slim'. Cheating on SAS selection is extremely difficult to get away with. Candidates are not allowed to walk on any made-up surface such as a road for example, apart from crossing it directly. And the D.S. made a habit of covertly positioned themselves along the routes to detect any digressions from the rules. Bergens were weighed at the beginning of each day, and at most checkpoints. Directing staff would often intercept candidates on their routes and carry out random weight checks.

There was, of course, an honourable and honest solution for me. I could, quite simply, have declared that I was not up to the task and I would have to accept failure. On the other hand, I could go for the 'cheating' option and hope for a much more palatable outcome.

I had a plan. A plan that was not without risk, but it was a risk I was willing to take, and I would implement it as soon as the higher weight was imposed at the beginning of test week.

Firstly, I applied three layers of heavy-duty, black masking tape to the back surface of my Bergen, overlapping onto the top edge. This would help it to skim along anything other than an incline, without getting snagged on certain surfaces, such as wet grass. Inside I carried a two-metre length of rope with clips on either end, which I could clip onto my waistband, in order to drag the rucksack along, in the manner of an Arctic explorer.

Secondly, I carried two five-litre cans which could be filled with water in the morning, and emptied after the initial weight check. Jettisoning the water would lighten my load by about twenty pounds. The cans would then be filled from a stream once I was approaching a checkpoint.

Finally, to cover the eventuality of a random check en route, I attached a piece of dirty, brown chord, about a foot long, to the bottom of my Bergen.

It was painful, but I made it through to test week, and we were now down to about thirty. What lay ahead of me was a hideous combination of routes across the most inhospitable parts of the Welsh countryside. I was beginning to hate Wales with a passion – it was totally beyond me why anyone on earth would want to lay claim to land that had gravity-defying bogs on the sides of fucking great hills that only ever seemed to go up.

Test week would culminate with 'endurance'. An agonising route of forty miles, carrying a fifty-five pound Bergen, plus all the rest of the crap, and the route had to be completed within twenty-four hours. In my case, I planned to drag the load for most of the way, and even then, it would weigh twenty pounds less than it should have done. Cheating was risky but I felt I had no other option since the blisters on my shoulders and back were raw and painful. A fifty-five-pound rucksack would soon become an unbearable burden.

For the first few days, my plan worked like a dream. Being able to drag my, much lighter, load along for a good deal of the route gave my shoulders and back some, very welcome relief.

It wasn't until halfway through 'endurance', frustratingly close to the end, that my plan began to fall apart.

According to my map, I had only two hundred metres, or so, to go to a small re-entrant, likely to contain a stream, where I could replenish my water cans. I would then have to carry the full load for only about a mile to my next checkpoint.

Suddenly, as if from nowhere, out of the drizzle, appeared an SAS soldier with a set of weighing-scales in his hands.

'Hang on mate. Just need to check the weight. Won't keep you a sec,' he said.

Fortunately, I was not doing my impression of 'Scott of The Antarctic' at the time. For maximum dramatic effect, I slid my thirty-five-pound load very slowly from my shoulders, trying my best to make it look as heavy as possible.

"What's all the tape for mate?" he asked suspiciously. Holding the scales out ready for me to put the carrying handle over the hook.

"Stops it rubbing into my back. Got a few blisters," I mumbled whilst adopting my best pained expression.

As he started to lift the scales with both hands, I trapped the dirty piece of chord, which I had attached earlier in the week, firmly under my boot.

The indicator needle on the scales passed slowly through thirty – forty

– fifty. Thankfully as soon as it went past fifty-five he released the load and I gave a huge sigh of relief. Without another word, he unhooked the scales and disappeared, like a spectre into the swirling mist.

What a fucking result, I thought to myself. Stifling a shriek of victory.

Who said cheats never prosper? Cheating had got me through my pilot's course, and now it looked as if it was going to get me through SAS selection.

I filled up my water cans at the babbling brook, humming a gentle refrain to myself. After that I, not only carried my Bergen in the prescribed manner, but I carried the full weight and put up with the pain.

I have no idea how long it took me to finish the notorious 'endurance' march, but it must have been in less than twenty-four hours.

The following morning, I was one of only twelve remaining candidates who was told that we had passed selection. We would be 'badged' once we had finished our continuation training and the 'combat survival course'.

CHAPTER TWENTY-TWO

"Bend over ... More!" A deep voice from behind me said as I stood completely naked. 'Touch the floor you dog'.

A finger was pushed roughly inside me and prodded about. At least I assumed, and certainly hoped, it was a finger.

A pair of hobnail boots with no laces, a rough pair of hessian trousers and an old Army greatcoat were thrown at my feet. The same voice, which had a distinct Russian accent, gave the order. "Put these on. Get into the back of the truck."

The boots were about three sizes too big for me, flopping about as I walked. I had to hold the trousers up with one hand – too big again, and no belt.

A piece of paper, with the figure '6' scribbled on it, was slapped onto the front of my greatcoat as I struggled to climb into the back of the windowless van.

"Sit. No talking," ordered the Russian as he slipped a black hood over my head, pulling the drawstring tightly around my neck, and plunging me into total darkness.

It was cold. Very cold. The middle of March and the van rocked violently as if it were being driven, not along a road, but along a rough unmaintained track. My, recently violated, arse was being jarred against the cold metal floor of the vehicle and my body constantly bashed against the sides and other bodies.

We came abruptly to a halt, throwing me forward, as the back door was opened and cold air rushed in. There was the sound of scuffling as if someone or something was being removed, or perhaps taken on board, before the door slammed shut.

At the sixth stop, I was grabbed by the shoulders and dragged towards the open door. I clung on to my trousers with one hand and tried to hold on to my oversize boots with the other, but my right one slipped away. I felt a moment of terror as I was launched into space before thudding onto the hard ground.

As I staggered to my feet the hood was ripped from my head. I blinked, still in darkness as I desperately tried to focus on something – anything – to try to overcome my disorientation.

The back of the van came into focus, starting to pull away into the night with the door still open. Suddenly my breath was taken away, and I fell to my knees in pain, as my right boot crashed into my chest.

With the vehicle gone I was left in absolute silence and a claustrophobic darkness. The sky was completely obscured by cloud, what we pilots would call 'eight-eighths cover', and I therefore stood very little chance of getting any sense of direction.

I decided to walk with the wind on my back, mainly because, that way the greatcoat gave me extra protection, albeit still meagre.

Although I didn't know exactly where I was, there were a few things that I did know.

I knew that if I could cross the main road, which lay about thirty miles to the south-west, then I would be out of enemy territory and would have reached freedom. Anyone this side of that main road was to be considered an enemy and must be avoided at all costs. I also knew that by first light there would be a Hunter Force in the area, intent on tracking me down. Dozens of troops who knew the ground well and trained in the art of tracking, would not only have dogs but would also have helicopters equipped with thermal imaging cameras in support. With the capability and determination of the Hunter Force and only one direction for me to go towards freedom, the odds of me avoiding capture were, well and truly, stacked against me.

It was bitterly cold and I had eaten nothing for more than twenty-four hours. Physically I was in reasonable shape. Psychologically I was beginning to feel very distressed and vulnerable.

I decided that I had to stick to the low ground and keep walking until I could find some sort of shelter. Thankfully the heavy cloud cover didn't develop into rain. Progress was slow due to the ill-fitting boots and trousers but, after about an hour, I stumbled across a fence and a hedgerow, which I followed downhill. Eventually, there was a break in the fence-line connected by a gate, and I was in luck. The gate was tied shut with blue nylon cord.

With hands that would hardly function due to the intense cold, I managed to cut lengths of the chord on a stone and produce a pair of boot laces and two belts.

I scrapped together as many leaves and twigs as I could to use as my bed for the night, and crawled into the hedgerow. I eagerly awaited the first signs of the sun, which would not only show me which way I needed to go but might also bring me some warmth.

I had been lucky with the haberdashery, but not so with my inbuilt compass. The sun started to rise from exactly the opposite direction to that which I needed to be heading. I had no option. The only way for me to remain free from captivity, by getting out of the enemy-held territory, was for me to retrace the steps over, what progress I had made throughout the previous night.

Not long after the sun began to rise over the horizon, I heard the ominous sound of a helicopter approaching from the east.

When being observed from the sky, the first thing that will highlight the quarry's location to the hunter is movement. The second thing, assuming the aircraft has a thermal imaging capability, is the heat emitted from the body.

The hedgerow above me was dense, and I felt reasonably confident that it would provide enough insulation to absorb my heat-signature. If I could manage to lay still, then I felt that there was a good chance that I would go unnoticed. The helicopter passed directly overhead my overnight accommodation without any change of direction, giving me no indication that I had been spotted. As the sound of the aircraft waned into the distance, I decided that I had to make some headway towards my goal, thirty miles or so, to the south-west. The sky was again obscured by heavy clouds scudding towards the north-east, and threatening to turn to rain.

There were plenty of guidelines around me to help me with my orientation, so I had no doubt that I was heading in the right direction. The propensity of moss to grow on the north-facing sides of trees, the wind direction and the lines of the shadows, despite the sky being overcast, all helped me to maintain a, generally, south-westward bearing.

I stumbled, rather than ran, across the rough and boggy terrain towards the corner of a small copse of conifer trees, about two miles in the distance.

With less than three hundred metres to go to the sanctuary of the wood, I heard, once again, the sickening drone of the Hunter Force's eye-in-the-sky.

I immediately dived to the ground and curled up in a ball, pulling my greatcoat over my head in an attempt to disguise the shape of my body. As the predators flew away to the south and disappeared I felt a slight feeling of elation – they had been outsmarted. Once again, I thought, my knowledge of flying and observation from the air had won me the day, and I felt confident that my tactics had been enough to stop me from being seen. My arrogance was ill-founded. The eagle-eyed bastards had spotted me.

Just as I crossed the tree-line into the wood the rain started to fall.

Despite the small boost my spirits had been given by my recently successful performance in the art of illusion, I was in rag-order. The cold, now exacerbated by the heavy rain, was penetrating through to my core. My first-aid training made me well aware of the symptoms of hypothermia and exhaustion. I was tired, cold and hungry – very hungry, but I had not reached the verge of collapse, and I was shivering, so that was a good sign. Hunger was, without a doubt, my biggest problem. Whoever said that we humans can survive, quite comfortably, for three weeks without food was definitely talking through his arse. I was only on my third day without eating anything and I was already beginning to get desperate. Most of my thoughts were of food and I was constantly on the lookout for anything that could be eaten. I kept my eyes fixed to the ground in case I should stumble across a nest full of tasty eggs, and I even thought about eating leaves or grass, which I managed to convince myself must surely be full of nutrition if they were able to sustain sheep and horses.

The hunger pangs and the feelings of weakness throughout my body ground away at my general wellbeing, and I was tempted to simply lie down, try to get warm, and attempt to overcome my malaise by sleeping.

I had no doubt that trying to progress across open countryside during daylight hours was a futile exercise. Wooded areas were just too few and far between. By the time I could pick up the sound of the helicopter, I simply wouldn't have enough time to react and find adequate top-cover to hide under. I felt that I was left with only one option. I would have to lie-up during the day under the cover of any woods that I could find, and then try to make my run for freedom during the night.

I gathered together any fallen branches that I could find and, once again, scrapped up leaves and anything else that might provide some insulation. With my back wedged against a tree trunk I crawled under my accumulation. This time I waited, not for the sun to rise, but for it to fall, and allow darkness to provide me with the protection I needed.

CHAPTER TWENTY-THREE

Dogs! I could hear dogs barking in the distance. They sounded excited as if they had picked up the scent of a wounded prey and they were getting closer. Suddenly, the sound of their barking was drowned out by the overwhelming noise of a helicopter circling directly overhead.

My heart was thumping in my chest. What to do? If I broke cover and left the woods, then I would be spotted instantly by the pilot and crew. If I broke cover and remained under the canopy then I would be left with nowhere to go, and the Hunter Force, with their dogs, would be on to me within minutes. I decided that, by remaining as still as I could, under my makeshift hideaway then, with the rain possibly washing away my scent, I might have a chance of not being found.

With a dog growling and barking aggressively only inches from my ear, I realised that I was about to be taken prisoner. I felt my pathetic shelter being kicked into the undergrowth.

"Hands behind your back," screamed the guard, as he positioned his boot down onto the side of my face and pressed down – hard, forcing me to exhale a muffled groan of pain.

After another bone-jarring journey in the back of a truck, with a hood tightly secured over my head, I was lead through what sounded like a courtyard and into a building.

As my handcuffs were removed, there was not a sound.

Guards on either side of me, each holding one of my upper arms and wrists, lead me gently forwards.

"Stop," one of them whispered.

A door in front of me was opened and I was lead inside. Underfoot I heard and felt harsh gravel, and the room resonated with overpowering 'white noise'.

"Stand," whispered the same guard into my ear.

My hands were placed onto a cold brick wall in front of me, and my legs were pulled slightly apart and away from the wall so that I was leaning forward and supported by my arms.

"Stand," was the last word that I would hear from the guard, or anyone, for quite a while.

How long I was made to remain in that 'stress-position' for I have no idea. The 'white noise' was confusing me, and I was finding it difficult to have any awareness of time – or anything else for that matter. When I tried to ease the strain on my body by lowering one of my arms, it would be held by the guard, and carefully, in total silence, placed back against the wall.

I felt the gentle treatment of the guards more distasteful than the rough treatment of the Hunter Force, and I was convinced that my brain was slowly becoming addled.

Desperately, I tried to work out what day of the week it was, but I couldn't. What time of day it might be – not a chance there. I attempted to recite poems or songs from my past, but I lost the words. Even the most elementary nursery rhymes and poetry seemed to have slipped from my memory.

Suddenly, as if descending from another dimension, hands were laid upon me and guided me to sit on the gravel cross-legged. The hood was removed, and hands on either side of my head steered my eyes towards the ground. On my knees were two slices of dry bread, and to the side sat a tin mug, half-filled with water.

I greedily ate the bread and guzzled back the water. With no hands to direct me, I sat staring at the floor. For some strange reason, I was afraid to look behind me.

A short while later I was returned to the 'stress-position', and was struggling to hold on to my sanity.

The 'white noise' was remorseless. Now and again, from somewhere in the distance, I could make out voices, but no matter how hard I concentrated, it was impossible for me to understand what they were saying. Sometimes they seemed to be speaking in a language that I couldn't understand. At other times, I could grasp the odd word of English but, even then, nothing they said made any sense at all to me. I had heard of people in captivity being brainwashed by being exposed to some form of sensory deprivation. Perhaps, I thought, that was what was happening to me.

In an attempt to break away from the tedium of the stress-position I said, in a loud voice. "Toilet. Toilet," but nothing happened. Could it be that the guards had gone and left me unattended? I slowly lowered one of my arms, just as a test. Immediately the robotic hands descended upon me, holding my elbow and wrist, and gently placing my hand back against the wall.

I mumbled to myself, "Dig deep. Concentrate. This can't go on forever. If I can just hold on to who I am, and what I am doing here, then I will get through this without cracking up. And I can hold on for a long time without a piss anyway."

There were a couple more sumptuous meal breaks, when I could tuck into my favourite feast of two slices of bread, and relish the half-mug-full of water, which I tried to convince myself was actually a rather exquisite soupçon of burgundy wine. But it didn't work.

After a while my whole body began to shake, not so much from the cold, but more from the fact that my muscles were reacting to the constant strain and lack of movement.

Four hands attached themselves to me and turned me away from the wall. I was lead through a door which was then closed behind me, and the 'white noise' was gone. The silence and the warmth of the environment felt strangely confusing and unwelcome. There was a strong aroma of, freshly brewed, hot drinking chocolate.

The drawstring on my hood was loosened and light flooded into my eyes as it was removed.

Bewildered and blinking into the dazzling light, I slowly became aware of my surroundings.

I was in an office, standing in front of a desk. Sat behind the desk was a man dressed in a uniform, sporting three silver stars on each of his shoulder epaulettes. Bright lights standing either side of the man were glaring straight into my eyes.

"What is your name?" the man said, with no trace of an accent.

"Warrant Officer Riley," I answered quietly.

The interrogator's voice rose. "Are you stupid? I asked you, what is your name. It is important that you answer correctly."

"Patrick James Riley," I said as precisely as I could.

"And what is your rank?"

'Warrant officer," I replied.

Taking down notes, and with a calmer voice, he continued. "There now Mister Riley, that wasn't difficult, was it?"

"I cannot answer that question sir," I replied, knowing that, according to the Geneva Convention, the only details I was required to supply were my number, rank, name and date of birth.

All members of the armed forces, who were defined as 'prone to capture' such as aircrew or members of Special Forces, were instructed never to provide any other information.

"Are you being given enough to eat?" he asked as he lit a cigarette.

"I cannot answer that question sir," I again repeated.

"You really are stupid, aren't you?"

"I cannot answer that question sir."

The interrogator was beginning to look perplexed, almost angry. He picked up his mug and took a sip of the warm delicious-smelling chocolate.

"Would you like a drink of this?" he asked, placing the mug back onto the desk.

I glanced to my right as if something had caught my eye.

Momentarily he looked to his left, and in that instant, I grabbed the mug and took a hasty gulp.

Without hesitation a guard descended on me and snatched the drink from my grasp as I said with a smile, and with chocolate dripping from my chin.

"I cannot answer that question sir."

The captain or three-star general, whatever he was, was definitely not happy.

"Take him away. Give him a shower and remember he has already been fed," he bellowed.

I felt elated with my victory. A victory which may have appeared small, but to me it was massive, and I felt that I would now be able to cope with another session of the 'white noise' and the gravel without any problems.

Were my ears deceiving me? Did the cross-examining officer really say "Give him a shower"?

If he did, then I was about to get one with my hood on.

"Perhaps the showers were in another building," I thought to myself, as I was lead outside, bollock naked, apart from my shower cap.

I wasn't taken to a shower block. I was forced to lie face-down across two thick metal girders, one running across my chest and shoulders, and the other across my shin bones. I was tied spread-eagled to the girders, or perhaps they were rails of some kind, which were icy cold and cut painfully into my flesh.

As the guards walked away I strained to listen to their conversation.

"We can't leave the poor bugger there. There might be a train coming," one said in a whisper.

"Course we can. He won't come to any harm. Next train's not due till tomorrow morning," the other replied.

A door slammed, and there was silence. I was left naked and tied, face down to, what I then realised, was a railway line. A fucking railway line!

Any attempts to loosen my bonds were hopeless, they just made the plastic restraints cut further into my skin. It felt as if the wide metal beams were melding into me. I was desperately uncomfortable, bitterly cold, and scared.

Suddenly my discomfort dissolved. My priorities changed. I felt a slight vibration being transmitted through the railway lines. No – I had to be wrong, surely it couldn't be a train – I had to be imagining it – but I wasn't. As the vibration increased, I screamed. "Help. Help. For fuck's sake help me. There's a train coming!"

I heard a door slam and the guards running towards me. They immediately started to cut me free.

"Quick, I can see the headlights," one said as I was hauled to my feet and dragged towards the building.

For the next few seconds, I stood gasping for breath as I listened to the noise of the train increase and rattle past.

"Don't you dare tell anyone about this," hissed a guard as I was lead, less gently than normal, along what sounded like a corridor.

The warmth, the smell and the light, once again invading my eyes as my hood was removed, assured me that I was back in the interrogation room.

This time there was a young woman sat by the officer. She looked me up and down as she smiled. Her smile turning into a mocking laugh as she cast her eyes onto my, shrivelled and withdrawn, wedding-tackle.

Instinctively I tried to cover myself with my hands.

"Don't be shy, Mister Riley," said the interrogator. "You certainly don't have anything that my assistant hasn't seen before. Would you like to get dressed before we start?"

"I cannot answer that question sir," I said somewhat pitifully.

"Are the guards treating you with proper respect, sergeant major?" he asked as if concerned.

"I cannot answer that question sir," I repeated.

The assistant chirped up. "Take him away," she said.

My hood stayed off and I was lead into the office next door.

There was the familiar face of the officer commanding training wing, Major Paddy Baxter. "Well done Red," he said as he pointed to a bundle of clothes on the chair next to him. "Get dressed and go and get yourself something to eat."

The Combat Survival and Resistance to Interrogation phase of SAS selection was over, and I certainly wasn't sorry to have put it behind me!

CHAPTER TWENTY-FOUR

Having passed selection, I was now a newly 'badged' SAS trooper and had managed to come full circle in my career. After reaching the rank of warrant officer I was once again a private soldier, as I had been almost eighteen years earlier. But I was happy – very happy, and I was happier still as I left the commanding officer's office after my welcoming interview.

The C.O. had outlined the details of my new appointment as a badged member and I was hugely relieved to learn that I would not be required to sneak through jungles with an enormous Bergen on my back. Nor would I be expected to abseil down the side of a building and leap through a window, in an attempt to rescue some helpless hostages. At my stage of life, it seemed highly likely that any hostages would just have sympathy with me, and feel it be more appropriate for them to lead me out of the besieged building, to save me from tripping over and doing myself an injury. I don't think I was ever the type of person who was cut out to deal with a real, close-quarter terrorist threat. The mere thought of confronting someone armed to the teeth, and intent on killing me filled me with dread. I just instinctively knew that there would come a time, in any confrontation, when I would simply throw down my weapon, turn on my heels and run away screaming for help. (Not the sort of image the public at that time expected of a heroic, swashbuckling SAS trooper.) I was a married man with three children and a mortgage for goodness sake! The last thing I wanted to do was to get involved with slapping anyone around – let alone pumping bullets into someone.

It, therefore, came as a great relief, when I was told that I would not be joining one of the regiment's four Sabre Squadrons but, was instead to be posted to the Operational Research Department – better known to everyone as Ops Research. My new role would be to look at improving methods of dealing with the ever-present threat of aircraft hijacks.

The remit I was given was to liaise with the officer commanding Counter Revolutionary Warfare (CRW) wing and the operations officer, and produce proposals to improve the regiment's capabilities to deal with any hijack situation, on any type of aircraft, anywhere in the world. The hijacking of passenger jets was popular at that time. It was generally considered to be only a matter of time before the UK antiterrorist team would be called upon to deal with a life-threatening hostage situation.

The SP team trained regularly to improve the techniques required to storm an aircraft, with the use of a mock-up version of a standard modern-day passenger jet. Which was on the grounds of the Pontrilas Army Training Area just outside Hereford. The Ops Officer and I decided that it would, more than likely, be beneficial if the team were given access to real aircraft to practice with, and we would, therefore, need the cooperation of British Airways which was then a nationalised company. In due course a request was put forward through Group Headquarters and the Ministry of Defence, for a meeting with BA, a short while later a meeting was arranged to be held at their Headquarters in Queens Building, by Terminal 2, at London's Heathrow Airport.

Chairing the meeting was, the then, General Manager Operations BA – Douglas Newham. Douglas had been a Royal Air Force pilot with Bomber Command during the Second World War, and for his many exploits he had been awarded a Distinguished Flying Cross. We got along well together, and we would later become good friends. He made it clear to us that the prime minister of the day, Margaret Thatcher, had instructed him to provide us with whatever resources the company had to hand.

Before the meeting closed, and we all retired to the boardroom for lunch with the chairman, Sir John King, it was agreed that British Airways would make two things available to the regiment.

The first was access to any of the wide range of aircraft, then operated by them, for the unrestricted use of the UK antiterrorist team. Provided the company received reasonable notice, then an aircraft would be positioned onto an RAF airfield, normally Brize Norton in Oxfordshire, and left entirely at the regiment's disposal. The SP team would then be able to practice assault techniques in a much more realistic environment, than a prefabricated mock-up shell.

The second thing that was agreed, was that they would provide me with anything that I may need, in order for me to build up my cover to become a convincing airline pilot. We came up with the suggestion that if I received sufficient training, then I was likely to be able to get on board a hijacked aircraft, provided the negotiators could reassure the hijackers that a change of crew was necessary.

I managed to convince everyone around the table that to become a credible airline pilot, experienced on just about any type of airliner, would take much more than simply donning an appropriate uniform. Apart from learning to fly a wide range of aircraft, from the small turboprop boneshakers used for island-hopping around the UK, to the very latest 747 transcontinental jets and the supersonic Concorde, I would also need to become totally familiar with the everyday routines of an airline pilot. The only way to do that was to, effectively, become a British Airways Senior First Officer. And so, the stall was set for my next three years of employment as a private soldier, more often referred to as a 'Jundi', in the Special Air Service.

CHAPTER TWENTY-FIVE

Strange though it may seem, I found the introduction to my new life as an airline pilot somewhat exciting. Of course, I was still a soldier, as I had been throughout all my adult life, but I felt that I was about to embark on a new career. Not as a soldier, but as an 'actor'. And an actor is exactly what I would have to become since my whole connection with the airline industry would, of course, be a complete sham. I was convinced that if I were to play the role of Patrick James Riley, airline pilot then I would have to do it as meticulously as I possibly could. I knew that if ever I was thrust onto the stage in earnest, there would be no prompt to help me out, and any fumbling of my lines could result in desperate consequences, not only for me but possibly for many other people.

Doug Newham, who I later became good friends with, agreed with the concept of me becoming, for all intent and purposes, a full-time pilot employed by British Airways. Doug introduced me to Captain Mike Channing who was nominated to become my mentor in the early stages of my transition. He, in turn, introduced me to Flight Engineer Peter Robinson, who could cover for Mike whilst on flying duties. Both Mike and Peter took me under their wing and helped me to find my way around the huge complex of offices. They also lead me through the procedures to take up my new appointment as a qualified Royal Air Force pilot joining the company.

I spent a couple of days in and around the Queens Building, familiarising myself with the day-to-day things such as; carparking, administration offices, catering facilities, security and such like, and was then issued with an employee number and identity card. After being allocated the rank of Senior First Officer, indicated by three broad silver bands on each arm, I was issued with two full sets of uniform.

Mike Channing liaised with a chap from the UK Civil Aviation Authority by the name of Neil Monks, who arranged for me to be issued with a current Airline Transport Pilots' Licence. The specific aircraft type upon which I was supposedly qualified, and normally included in the licence, was intentionally left blank for me to simply fill in should it ever be necessary for me to produce it to a hijacker.

At that stage of my life, I was a reasonably well-qualified pilot with over five thousand flying hours under my belt, albeit with the clear majority of them on helicopters. As I strapped into the right-hand seat of the Lockheed L-1011 TriStar, I recalled that the last time I had flown a fixed-wing aeroplane was on my *ab initio* flying training with the Army Air Corps. The basic Army Pilot's course was in those days, undertaken on the de Havilland Chipmunk T10, a tiny two-seater piston-engine trainer weighing less than a tonne, and capable of cruising at around ninety knots.

The aircraft I was now strapping on to my back was enormous, weighing in at over two hundred tonnes and having a cruising speed in excess of five hundred knots. It felt to me as though I would be able to fit the tiny Chipmunk I had last flown into the cavernous cockpit of the fifty million pound TriStar airliner.

In the left-hand seat, with the flying checklist in one hand and a steaming cup of coffee in the other sat Captain Dave Martin. Dave was a large powerful man, ruggedly handsome, and with the top button of his shirt undone and sleeves rolled up, he looked more like he was about to start digging a trench than to supervise my flying. He hailed from Liverpool, where his father had once been Chief Constable. He was a no-nonsense sort of bloke with a booming laugh and a great sense of humour. "Ok, Red let's have a couple of circuits and bumps to start with. Just don't make the bumps too big and, for heaven's sake, don't bend the aeroplane or make me spill my coffee."

Dave received clearance to taxi to the hold of runway three one from the Air Traffic Control tower and gave me a nod as he nonchalantly took a sip from his beaker. Jim, the flight engineer sitting between us, and a little to the rear leant forward slightly and gave me a 'thumbs-up'.

I wasn't sure what I was supposed to do next – the huge array of instruments and switches in the cockpit seemed to overwhelm me and my mind suddenly went blank. Not wanting to look like a complete 'dick', I decided to give it my best shot and just pretend that I was once again in the tiny Chipmunk. With my right hand on the miniature steering wheel down by my right knee and my left hand on the three power-levers, I released the brakes by tapping my toes on the top of the rudder pedals. I gently eased the power levers forward simultaneously, and gradually the two hundred tonnes of metal and plastic started to move forward. As the enormous mass surrounding me started to gain momentum I panicked, and at that point I had two options. I could squeal for help or I could slam the brakes on, and I didn't hesitate to go for the latter.

Dave lurched forward spilling his precious hot coffee over his knees.

"What the fuck?" he exclaimed, tossing the checklist over his shoulder and frantically brushing the steaming liquid off his trousers. "We've not even got off the ground and you've managed to give me third-degree burns."

"I just thought I should check that the brakes were working," I muttered meekly.

Dave took a deep breath as if to calm himself. "Ok, so from now on let's assume that the brakes are working just fine. Remember momentum is equal to mass times velocity, and I guess you are dealing with a lot more mass than you are used to, so let's have another go."

I acknowledged Dave with a serious expression and a nod. Out of the corner of my eye, I could see Jim, with his head in his hands and his shoulders rocking as if he was trying to stifle uncontrollable laughter.

I managed to taxi out to the 'line-up and hold' point for runway Three-One by anticipating that the aircraft would take much more time and distance to respond than I would hitherto normally expect.

Having now recovered the discarded checklist Dave read out the pre-take-off checks. I responded to each item in turn and, with Jim's help, set the correct configuration ready for take-off.

Air Traffic Control passed the message, "Speedbird Two-Two you are clear to take-off."

It appeared to me that Dave had decided not to take any more chances. He knocked back the last dregs of his drink and placed the empty beaker in the cup-holder to his side.

The L-1011 TriStar was the first ever commercial airliner capable of flying from take-off to landing fully automatically, but today we were having none of that. Every phase of flight had to be done manually with me in control, and although I don't recall feeling nervous, I certainly would have had to concentrate intently.

"Right Red, let's go. Relax and enjoy the ride. Don't forget, it's only an aeroplane but I think you are about to find out why people call her 'The Queen of the Skies'," said Dave with a smile.

With Jim's hand on top of mine, I eased the power levers forward and slipped my feet from the brakes. As the speed started to increase I could control direction down the runway with my feet on the rudder pedals. I was a little bit wayward to start with, but it didn't take me long to be able to steer accurately along the runway centre line.

As Dave monitored the flight instruments he calmly called out each reference speed as we reached it. "Eighty knots – vee one – Rotate."

At this speed, I eased back on the yoke and, almost imperceptibly, The Queen of the Skies lifted into the air.

The TriStar was a beautiful aircraft to fly, being very responsive to any control inputs, and performing like a much smaller and manoeuvrable aeroplane.

Apart from a huge bounce on my first attempt at landing, which lead to a few classic, Liverpudlian expletives from the captain, I soon got the hang of things. Dave put my 'depth perception' problem down to me not being used to sitting so far up from the ground, and after a few circuits and bumps, I became reasonably proficient at flying my first wide-bodied passenger jet.

I was heartily congratulated by Dave and Jim later that evening in the bar as they presented me with a, quickly knocked-up certificate stating that I was now fully qualified to fly 'The Queen of the Skies', and ordered to get the next round of drinks in. Before leaving it was agreed that arrangements would be made back at Heathrow for me to make my debut trip 'down the line', with a recommendation to fly to Dar es Salaam and Kilimanjaro with a four-day stopover in Arusha. A trip that would, eventually, become a reality and would turn out to be extremely memorable, and not just for the flying.

CHAPTER TWENTY-SIX

My phone call to the British Airways Operations department, who were arranging my first long-haul trip for later that month, was interrupted by Bob Waters, the second-in-command of Ops Research. 'Just getting reports of a 737 hijack situation taking place right now and reported to be heading towards London,' he said seriously.

By the time I had grabbed my hold-all and flight bags and driven around to CRW, the SP team were lining up their vehicles and were, just about, ready to go. Corporal Dave Pearson, from the Intelligence Cell, was passing amongst us, confirming that a British aircraft had been taken by armed aggressors and was about to land at Stansted Airport, north-east of London. We were ordered to make our way there as quickly as possible.

The whole counterterrorist team, in a wide range of civilianised vehicles, left Hereford in a convoy with blue flashing lights and police sirens. So intent was the team on getting to the scene of the incident without delay, we didn't even stop at the 'greasy spoon' cafe on the A417, which was an almost compulsory ritual during any road trip to the capital.

In my hold-all, I had two complete sets of British Airways Pilots uniform, one for a captain and one for a senior first officer. I also had with me two, standard, black leather flight bags which had been modified by the 'Spookie' technicians at Fort Halstead not far from Milton Keynes. The bags had been fitted with listening devices to transmit any conversation from on board the aircraft back to the Incident Control Room.

If the police negotiators could manage to convince the hijackers that they would be allowed to fly away – provided they would agree to a change of the flight-deck crew, then I, plus one other 'pilot', would get on board with the modified flight bags. Rest assured dear reader that the plan was never for me to get on board and save the day, in a blaze of glory. Taking out the terrorists single-handedly with deadly jabs and kicks, fashionable at that time with the likes of James Bond, or Bodie and Doyle from *The Professionals*, was certainly not for me. Once on board, my job would be simply to pass as much intelligence as possible back to the team prior to them storming the aircraft.

Over the past few weeks, we had worked out a system of codes by using veiled-speech and the aircraft transponder, to give the team their best chance of a successful outcome. How many terrorists? How many weapons? Are any of the doors booby-trapped? Is there any evidence of explosives? My responsibility was simply to keep talking and try to paint a picture of the situation on board. With any luck, I would be able to indicate whether the hostage-takers might be becoming agitated and therefore extremely dangerous.

Upon arrival at the airport, we were marshalled into a holding area which was well out of sight of the hijacked aircraft. The aircraft was a British Airways 737 and had been taken over whilst on a flight from Tunisia to Edinburgh with one hundred and sixteen passengers and crew on board, most of them returning from holiday. It was thought, but my no means certain, that there were three armed men involved and they had taken control of the holiday jet just before entering the airspace of the UK.

Apparently, one man, armed with a pistol, had held the gun at the captain's head and demanded that they turn back and land at Houari Airport on the northern coast of Algeria. The crew managed to convince the man that they had insufficient fuel to do that, and they would have to land at London to refuel before they could attempt the trip back to Algiers. The captain had then discreetly selected the transponder code indicating to Air Traffic Control that the aircraft had been hijacked, and soon after that requested an immediate landing at London Stansted. Upon receipt of the transponder code, the Senior Air Traffic Controller had alerted the police who, in turn, contacted the Ministry of Defence.

Plans had been in place for some time with the UK authorities to deal with a situation such as this and it was then a policy that in the event of a hijack, attempts would be made to steer the aircraft towards a landing at Stansted Airport. There an area had been designated for parking the aircraft and an Operations Centre had been set up with the necessary reception areas and facilities for the police and the SP team to rehearse and prepare for a possible storming of the aircraft.

At that time, I had no idea whether a change of crew would be negotiated and I would be required to take on my new acting role, but I had to be prepared. Whilst trying to keep my 'stage-fright' under control and appear calm and confident at all costs, I looked around for someone who might be willing to come on board with me as the second crew member. Mick Gold had been brought into CRW in a most unusual way. He had been recruited directly from civilian life to make use of his highly impressive fighting skills and had become the regiment's unarmed combat expert and adviser. He had recently spent time with me working on how I might best be able to deal with an armed aggressor within the confines of a cockpit. As you are by now aware, I was never the sort cut out to be involved with taking out murderous terrorists with my bare hands, nevertheless what Mick had taught me did leave me feeling quietly confident that if the situation ever arose I would be able to make a pretty good fist of things. Ideally, a qualified pilot would have been asked to volunteer to join me but no one in the vicinity fitted that bill. I decided to ask 'fighter' Mick. Not because of his knowledge of hijack situations, or because of his fighting skills. It was purely because he was, more-or-less, the same size as me and I only had one spare uniform available.

Despite not knowing the first thing about how to fly a large passenger jet, Mick volunteered without hesitation. We donned our uniforms and stuffed our modified flight bags with flying paraphernalia while at the same time I brought my new co-pilot up to speed, as far as I could, with the code system I had worked out with the Control Room staff. We waited, rather nervously, and watched with interest to see how things would develop.

About an hour before last light the police negotiators agreed to send food and drinks on board and steps were put in place by the front left door. As the door opened one hijacker, holding an AK-47 was photographed and identified as the leader, who called himself Achmed. The food trays, two of which had discreet transmitters built into them, were taken into the aircraft and the door was quickly closed.

As darkness descended the lead terrorist and spokesman became very agitated and threatened to start shooting the passengers unless the aircraft was provided with fuel immediately. The authorities, once again, agreed to the demands and the aircraft was topped up with enough fuel to provide more than sufficient range to fly to Algiers.

A little while later, Achmed could be heard screaming at the pilots. Telling them to start-up, take-off and set course towards Africa at once. Both the Captain and the First Officer were heard making excuses, insisting that they were too exhausted and distressed to fly and they were unwilling to put the lives of all the innocent passengers at risk.

Suddenly a shot rang out. A few seconds later the plane's door was opened and the body of, what appeared to be a man in uniform, was placed on the top of the steps. Two members of the team were allowed to recover the body, which was then identified as the young British Airways first officer.

At this point, it was decided that the lives of the hostages were now in real and imminent danger and control of the situation was handed over to the senior military commander on the scene. Negotiations were continued with Achmed and it was agreed that a fresh Flight Deck crew, who would be willing to fly to Algeria, would come on board provided the women and children would be permitted to disembark.

The exchange was agreed and Mick and I were told to slowly approach the aircraft steps. With about twenty yards to go a male wearing jeans and T-shirt and a bandana around his forehead appeared at the top of the steps wielding an AK-47. The gunman, who I assumed to be Achmed, aimed his weapon directly at Mick and myself. We both stopped instantly.

"No bags. No bags," shouted Achmed.

"No need to shout, shithead. We're not fucking deaf," whispered Mick as we both placed our flight bags on the ground.

"One man only. Hands up. Come. Come," screamed the hijacker.

I put my hands in the air and started to move forward, just able to make out what my co-pilot was muttering under his breath.

'If he shouts at you again mate give him a good kick in the balls like I taught you.'

At the top of the stairs, the gunman nodded at me as if ordering me to stop. Not wanting to make him angry again I thought it best to play it safe, so I stopped. With Achmed's weapon pointing directly at my chest a second male, looking remarkably like the first, came out of the aircraft and, after patting me down, lead me into the empty cockpit. I sat in the left-hand seat, which would normally be occupied by the captain, and cast my eye around the multitude of dials and switches. The Auxiliary Power Unit was running and electricity was being supplied to the radios and transponder which were already switched on.

A few minutes later I was joined by Mick who took up his place in the right-hand seat, still mumbling under his breath. I got the impression that he was not very happy about being pushed around – something that he was, definitely not used to. Nevertheless, he managed to give me a cheery smile as he strapped himself into the co-pilot's seat.

Glancing back towards the main cabin I could see several women and children, led by the real captain, leaving the aircraft. Both of us sitting in the flight deck were constantly trying to ascertain as to whether there were more terrorists than the two we had already seen. This information would be vital for the team and I had to pass as much, up to date and confirmed intelligence as possible, back to the control room.

"How many?" I whispered to Mick.

"Two definites," he replied.

"Doors?" I whispered again.

"Clear," he acknowledged.

I selected the figures Two and Zero on the transponder, indicating to the team, now preparing to storm the aircraft, that there were two confirmed armed terrorists and no doors appeared to be booby-trapped.

The first gunman came back into the cockpit, this time followed by a young woman wearing a white blouse, black trousers, and carrying a 9mm Browning pistol.

I discreetly changed the figure Two on the transponder to a Three.

"Fly us to Algiers now or you will all be killed." shouted Achmed.

"Ok," I said, as calmly as I could. "We need to find the correct charts and get the aircraft ready. Which will take a few minutes, and then we can go."

"Five minutes only. Then we kill a passenger," he said, in his loud annoying manner.

I started up the engines whilst trying to sound as professional as possible by saying things like, "ignition" or "temperatures and pressures rising", to which Mick gave replies such as "roger" or "correct", almost as if he had some idea of what was going on.

I requested taxi instructions from what sounded like the Air Traffic Control Tower, but was in fact the Incident Operations Room.

"You are cleared to taxi for runway Zero-Four to hold for a departure to Algiers," came the very convincing response.

"We are now ready to take-off for Algiers. Would everyone please be seated with their seatbelts fastened," I said, rather pompously.

And to my surprise, everyone, including the gunmen, did exactly as they were told.

I released the brakes and eased the power levers forward to overcome the aircraft's inertia and gradually increase speed as we began to taxi towards the main runway.

There was only the sound of the engines. An unmistakable tension existed between Mick and I as we sat staring straight ahead waiting for the pre-arranged trigger signal, which we knew was coming.

The windshield suddenly burst into a blinding white light as a powerful beam was directed momentarily into our eyes.

Instantly I slammed on the brakes and switched off the main electrics, plunging the whole aircraft into total darkness. Almost immediately the whole fuselage began to shudder violently as helicopters landed, one on each wing. Seconds later, the cabin doors were flung open and huge explosions and disorientating flashes surrounded the aircraft. For about thirty seconds, absolute mayhem reigned in and around the aircraft with explosions and barking dogs on the outside and shots ringing out from inside the darkened cabin.

I flicked the electrics back on to illuminate the whole aircraft and, thereby, indicate to everyone in the cabin that the exercise had now come to an end.

The time had arrived for everyone involved to sit around and discuss what, if anything, went wrong. Certainly, not for the reason of pointing the blame at any single individual, but rather to try to learn from our mistakes.

Exercises were a very important part of our training schedule and reality was an essential part of any exercise. Role players would be selected for their ability to portray the characteristics of the terrorists we were most likely to come up against at that time, be they Palestinians, Iranians, Spanish, German or Irish.

No one was ever criticised for making a mistake during an exercise or any other form of training we undertook. But any errors were brought to light purely in order for every member of the team to try to try to avoid repeating those errors. As we all sat around, it was pointed out that the replacement co-pilot's trousers looked ridiculously short – 'fighter Mick' was about two inches taller than me. To my horror, the question was then asked 'Why was the captain wearing a G10 Army issue wristwatch'?

Not much I could say to that other than "Sorry, I fucked up."

Not long after the meeting I went out and bought myself a, rather expensive, all singing and dancing, 'Pilot's Chronometer', which I kept in the pocket of my British Airways uniform ready for me to wear for my next performance at a hijacking. Little did I know that my next performance would not be in London, but in somewhere far more dangerous. And any wardrobe malfunctions at this one were likely to cost me a lot more than a little embarrassment at a post-exercise debrief.

Training with the counter terrorist team in Hereford, April 1980

Me and Don Craven preparing for our 'three-legged'
climb up Mount Kilimanjaro

Memento given to members of the team after
storming the Iranian Embassy in London 1980

Me at the controls of a Scout Helicopter before
running out of fuel near Oxford

Head of anti-hijack UK, in deep cover as a British Airways pilot

At the controls of a Sioux helicopter, Northern Ireland 1979

Basic training Catterick Camp, Yorkshire 1964

Blue team outside the 'Embassy', Pontralis.
Me kneeling with my arm on Fred's shoulder

My brother Howard with Lady DI at the Terrence Higgins Trust, London

Howard before he became ill, Florida

Me in my cowboy suit with my sisters and brother ©1950

On the ranges with MI6, Gosport

Prince Charles, Molly and myself in the
Segeant's Mess 22 SAS, Hereford 1981

CHAPTER TWENTY-SEVEN
HEAD OF UK ANTI-HIJACK TEAM

It felt to me as though it was really important for me to endeavour to learn every aspect of the job of an airline pilot, in order to enable me to play my new role in life convincingly. I arrived at London Heathrow in plenty of time for me to park my car in the staff carpark, and then to spend some time soaking up the atmosphere of the operational side of the airport.

I met up with Ron Hale, the L-1011 training captain who I had been scheduled to fly with on my first British Airways 'Line Duty'. A trip which would take me to Kilimanjaro via Dar es Salaam, with a four-day stopover in Arusha, and then back, via the same route to London.

I shadowed Ron as he went through all the flight planning procedures; checking the en route weather, the aircraft load sheets, technical logs, fuel certificates etc. I sat next to him as he supervised the crew briefing, introducing me as Senior First Officer Red Riley, a newly arrived, but experienced pilot. Ron was the only member of the crew who was aware of my true identity and role.

I felt that it was going to be interesting to see if any crew members considered me to be not-quite-right after spending the next five days with me. My cover story was that I had just recently joined the company after leaving the Royal Air Force where I had been flying C-130 cargo planes.

I walked around the immense passenger jet in the wake of the captain, checking for any damage or irregularities. Once on board we ran through the list of pre-flight checks, started the engines, and then we were on our way.

The techniques required to fly any sort of aeroplane are very much the same once the thing is off the ground. Apart from the variation in speed of the different types, getting from A to B is simply a matter of what aid you choose to use. Be it the 'mark-one eyeball' and a map, ground located navigational beacons or airborne devices such as Inertial Navigation Systems (INS) or Global Positioning Systems (GPS). On modern aircraft, these systems can be interfaced with the automatic pilot. Navigation, to anywhere on the planet, is simply then a matter of feeding information into a computer via a keypad, making sure that the autopilot is engaged, and then pressing the 'Direct To' button.

Most pilots have a tendency to wave their arms around the cockpit, and press a few buttons to check and cross-check. Not really essential, of course, but it helps to impress the cabin-staff and allows the aircrew to display their importance. I have always thought that the aircraft systems are extremely reliable and accurate, and they tend to go wrong only when overzealous pilots start fiddling about unnecessarily.

The stewardess who brought lunch into us was particularly attractive. I couldn't help myself. Suddenly, as if with a mind of their own, my arms were waving about the cockpit, and I made sure that she noticed just what a sterling job I was doing of, not only ensuring that everything was checked, but also cross-checked.

Once we had eaten I volunteered to take the lunch trays back into the galley, where I was, very much, hoping to bump into the attractive stewardess.

Her name was Hilary. She was married, no children, living in Wimbledon and had worked for the airline for about ten years. She was stunning. I would have liked to have told her that I wasn't just an ordinary pilot, but I was, in fact, some sort of secret agent and was only on board to protect her and the rest of the passengers and crew. But, of course, I couldn't. I just had to hope that my involuntary arm swinging, and checking had been enough to leave a lasting impression on her.

I did give her my rehearsed story about having been in the RAF, single – naturally – and living in a pleasant country cottage just outside St Albans.

I must have been making progress. She asked me if I would be going to the usual room-party, once we had arrived at the hotel in Arusha. I, of course, told her that I would be there since I had never been known to miss any sort of party.

I stepped back into the flight deck with a smile on my face and suppressing the urge to give a huge 'fist-bump', accompanied with a "Yes", just in case the Captain came to the opinion that I was not taking this job seriously enough. The TriStar L-1011 was capable of landing fully automatically but, as we arrived at the 'top of descent' for Kilimanjaro International Airport (KIA), the captain asked me take over control and carry out a VFR, manual landing. In other words, land the aircraft without referring to any navigation aids, and without using the automatic pilot or the auto-throttles.

The higher and hotter a runway is, the faster the approach-to-landing speed needs to be. With KIA being at three thousand feet above sea level, and the temperature at ground level on that day getting close to thirty degrees centigrade, the approach speed was going to be relatively fast. I calculated it to be one hundred and fifty knots on the final approach, and one hundred and forty knots as the wheels touched the ground; what was known as the threshold speed.

On the final approach, I set the aircraft up with the runway directly ahead of me and asked the non-handling pilot to extend the flaps, thereby decreasing the stalling speed. I then called for the undercarriage to be lowered in preparation for landing. At this stage, we discussed, and agreed upon, a missed-approach procedure. This would be carried out if, for whatever reason, we were unable to land at the last minute. On that day, with no other traffic in the vicinity, we agreed to simply carry out a circuit to the right at three thousand feet, and fly around the airport to try again.

Normally, when on approach, the speed appears to increase as the ground gets closer, but it is vital that the airspeed is maintained. Dropping below the threshold speed too early could lead to a sudden loss of lift close to the ground, and therefore become extremely dangerous.

I concentrated on keeping the aircraft straight and aiming to arrive at the end of the runway at the calculated speed. When Ron called out "fifty feet", I gently eased back the throttles and the control column simultaneously to 'flare' the aircraft (raise the nose and reduce the speed), to make contact with the surface at one hundred and forty knots exactly.

The moment all the wheels were on the ground I pushed the control column forward and lifted the throttle levers up and back to apply reverse thrust, causing the whole aircraft to shudder as the speed decreased. At sixty knots, I cancelled the reverse-thrust and taxied towards the airport terminal.

Ron and the flight engineer congratulated me on a job well done – my first landing with a load of fare-paying passengers on board.

CHAPTER TWENTY-EIGHT

As we were getting out of the crew bus at the hotel in Arusha, I picked up my own bag and then went to carry Hilary's, before being reminded by the captain, as he shook his head, "Flight deck crew do not carry stewardess's bags, no matter how pretty they are."

Duly reminded of the need for me to act out my role as realistically as possible, I put the bag down and left her to carry it herself.

It turned out that Hilary's bag was packed full with miniature bottles of alcohol from the onboard bar, which was heartily drank later that evening at the opening-night room-party.

We both got along really well together and, after leaving the party, we joined two or three other members of the crew for a spell of midnight skinny-dipping.

With me dressed only in a pair of boxer-shorts and Hilary dressed only in a towel, we kissed goodnight. Instead of going into my room I was invited into the room next-door-but-one, for a small brandy as a nightcap.

Over the past twenty years, or so, I had had the good fortune to be able to fly, just about, every type of aircraft. There wasn't enough room in the 'Types Flown' section of my log book to list them all. From tiny microlights, through helicopters and autogyros to fast jets, airliners and even the supersonic Concorde.

Whilst under instruction I was lead to believe that I had, what was known in the trade, as 'a great pair of hands'. This meant that I could 'feel' whatever I was flying, through the air. Rather than having to resort to memorising, and trying to set arbitrary figures; pitch angles, speeds, power settings and angles of bank, all seemed to come naturally to me rather than me spouting off numbers and then struggling to set them accurately. Over many thousands of flying hours, and across a hugely diverse range of flying machines, my 'great pair of hands' had finally superseded, even my 'excellent feet'.

Now in total darkness, and with nothing to keep me 'on target', other than my sense of feel, I am fighting to maintain control. Only, by summoning every ounce of concentration available to me, am I able to keep things moving in the right direction.

The gentle movement of my fingers must be maintained at just the right tempo. The amount of pressure I apply is crucial – too much could be even worse than too little. Most important of all is, keeping the damned, elusive 'button' under control. Any excessive movement in this slippery environment and it could be lost – like a bar of soap in the bath.

Everything was going well. She grabbed my wrist to make sure that my hand stayed, right where it was, and I didn't allow the 'soap' to slip away at this crucial time.

'Yes... yes,' she gasped, arching her back and pressing her bum hard against my stomach.

I was now in the final stages of the 'glide-path', pushing up inside her.

Her orgasm seemed to take control of her whole body. The uncontrolled spasms emphasised by staccato gasps, and squeals of delight.

I shuddered to a halt.

'Fucking hell'. We gasped in unison, before cracking up into fits of laughter.

CHAPTER TWENTY-NINE

The next morning, I was faced with a small problem. How to avoid being seen leaving the wrong hotel room, dressed in only a pair of boxer shorts, when most of the crew were staying along the same corridor as we were. My room was only two doors away, but my new paramour didn't want me to risk giving the game away to her workmates – after all, she was a respectable married woman.

It wasn't long before I came up with another one of my dastardly plans.

There was a narrow ledge below the window, which ran across the entire length of the building. Fortunately, I could see that the window of my room had been left open. I suggested that I climb down onto the ledge, manoeuvre sideways along it and then jump up into my room. Meanwhile, she could leave, without worrying about bumping into anyone and make her way down for breakfast with the rest of the crew.

Hilary was reassured when I told her that I had done a considerable amount of rock-climbing during my days with the RAF Mountain Rescue Team in Wales.

I lowered myself very carefully onto the ledge, which now seemed to be much narrower than it at first looked, and gingerly started to slide sideways towards the second window.

At the same time, Hilary left her room and walked down the corridor and towards the restaurant. The waiter guided her towards the large table which had been reserved for British Airways and was set outside by the swimming pool. Around the table sat Captain Hale and his crew – apart from two.

As Hilary sat down to join them the Captain looked up at the side of the accommodation block. "Isn't that our First Officer Red crawling along the side of the building in his underpants?" he said, pointing with his spoon.

The cat was well and truly out of the bag when Hilary didn't look up but covered her face with her hands instead.

I climbed up and jumped through the second window. To my horror, it was not my room. I was in a storeroom with sheets and cleaning materials stacked all around me. Fortunately the door was unlocked and I was able to get into the corridor.

At the reception desk, with a sheet draped across my shoulders, I explained that I had locked myself out of my room and was given another key.

A few minutes later, when I nonchalantly rolled up at the swimming pool for breakfast, I was greeted with a lot of smiling faces and a modest ripple of applause.

My relationship with Hilary lasted for a couple of years after our trip to East Africa. We would get together, mainly, when I managed to manoeuvre my way onto routes she was scheduled to be flying. The most memorable ones being a four-day stopover to Vancouver and Seattle, or a week-long trip to Perth via Singapore, when she had later transferred to the 747 fleet.

But all good things must come to an end. When her husband became suspicious and threatened her with divorce, she decided that I would have to go. So, I did. And my round-the-world love affair was promptly concluded when a letter, addressed to Red the Pilot SAS Hereford, somehow found its way, to my office. A colleague from work decided to do me a favour and deliver the letter to my home. Which he did – whilst I was away and my wife was happily preparing dinner for her devoted husband.

When I walked into my house I was met by a less-than-happy spouse.

"Hilary. Never heard of her," I spluttered. Tossing the letter to one side. "Either she is some sort of mad fantasist or some knob-head at work is trying to stitch me up."

I'm not sure, whether or not my wife ever believed me. She did at least, however, give me the benefit of the doubt, and gave me the impression that she accepted my story.

Marriage break-ups and divorces were very common throughout the Special Forces Group. Perhaps they could best be blamed upon the long, and numerous, periods of separation most couples were exposed to. I, for one, was certainly 'married to the job', and would never want to miss any bit of action that might be taking place anywhere in the world. Without any hesitation, I would volunteer to get involved regardless of any stress my family may be subjected to.

I managed to hang on to my marriage, by a thread, throughout the whole of my military career.

It was not until I started to work for MI6 that the, almost inevitable, divorce papers started to change hands.

CHAPTER THIRTY
HEREFORD ENGLAND, 14 JUNE 1985,
1940 HOURS

The party, to celebrate my thirty-ninth birthday, was in full swing. Nothing too elaborate, just a few friends and neighbours joining us at my home in Moreton-on-Lugg.

Above the normal party chatter, and the sound of Abba blaring out their famous hit 'Waterloo', a female voice yelled out from the hallway.

"Red! Someone at the door for you. Invite him in – and tell him he could ring my bell anytime!" she said, with a giggle.

After pushing my way through the dancers, and the boisterous drinkers, I was confronted by a handsome young man in full SAS uniform. At that time, it was rather unusual to leave camp dressed in anything other than civilian clothes. There was then a serious threat of attack from members of the IRA, or even just from being photographed by some overenthusiastic newspaper reporter.

The soldier, dressed as he was, and turning up at my front door at eight o'clock on a Friday night, meant that he, almost certainly, had something serious to say.

"Uncle Sam requests the pleasure of your company," he said with a smile.

"What, right this minute?" I asked, as I hitched up my white flared trousers, which I had dug out especially for the occasion.

"Yep. If not sooner," he replied. "Was told to remind you to bring all your airline pilot's kit with you – let's go."

Without another word or any explanation to anyone at the party, I jumped into the waiting vehicle.

Rather appropriately, Abba was, by then, banging out 'Hasta Mañana', as we sped out of the close, and down the A49 towards Stirling Lines.

I, of course, had no idea what tomorrow was about to bring.

Upon arrival at 'the Lines', I was met by a captain who I had not met before since he had just recently passed selection and joined G Squadron. He was accompanied by a signaller, who I was also unfamiliar with, holding on to a huge suitcase which I was told held the very latest, state-of-the-art Satellite Communication System.

We were told that a helicopter was standing by, ready to take us to Royal Airforce Station Northolt, in London, and that I should collect my kit, and expect to be fully briefed once we were in the air.

"Nice trousers," shouted the captain as I rushed across the square into my office.

I quickly grabbed my British Airways paraphernalia, which I always kept ready to go and started to leave. Just then, as if by magic, I spotted a change of clothes, belonging to Bob Waters, the second-in-command of Ops Research, left on the desk next to mine, and they included a pair of jeans which were only a few sizes too big. Nothing that a tight belt and a couple of turn-ups couldn't cope with – and anything was better than the embarrassing white 'seventies flares'.

Sitting in the back of the Agusta 109 helicopter, which had been 'liberated' from the Argentine Airforce after the Falklands war, and was now used by the SAS Flight, I was briefed by the captain.

Earlier in the day a Boeing 727 operated by Trans World Airlines (TWA) had been hijacked shortly after taking off from Athens.

TWA Flight 847 was en route from Cairo to San Diego with scheduled stops in Athens, Rome, Boston and Los Angeles. Two armed men, thought to be members of the Middle-Eastern group Hezbollah, had taken over control of the aircraft and forced the pilot, Captain John Trestrake, to land in Beirut. Most of the passengers and all the crew were believed to be American citizens. There were also thought to be several British subjects on board. Since American interests far outweighed those of the United Kingdom, the US counterterrorist team, and not the British SAS, had been tasked to take overall command and prepare to deal with the situation.

The 1st Special Forces Operational Detachment-Delta (1st SFOD-D), commonly referred to as Delta Force, had been alerted and were then in transit to a Forward Operating Base (FOB) close to the incident. RAF Akrotiri in Southern Cyprus had been nominated as the FOB.

The Delta Force Operations Officer at that time was Lt Colonel Lewis (Bucky) Burruss. Bucky was someone who I knew well, having worked with him on many occasions. I had recently visited him in his base in North Carolina, and Bucky would often come over to visit us in Hereford or London. His liaison trips were, primarily, undertaken to exchange operating methods and techniques but, more often than not, descended into nothing more than a piss-up with myself and Crocker. We spent many happy times together behaving outrageously in the Special Forces Club, or in the sergeant's mess of 21 SAS, who were then based on the Kings Road just off Sloane Square. The person in charge of the mess, at that time, was Regimental Sergeant Major Rover Slatery, an SAS veteran, who put up with us only because he himself had bad behaviour down to an art form.

As soon as Bucky had been told about the hijacking, he had immediately put in a request, through the Pentagon and the Ministry of Defence, for me to attend the incident. Quite remarkably, the United States had no one, at that time, with Special Forces status, who was trained to fly commercial airliners.

CHAPTER THIRTY-ONE

After touching down at RAF Northolt, Ben the signaller said that he needed to confirm that the SatCom was working correctly before we left the country. The captain and I agreed that twenty minutes, or so, on the ground would be much appreciated, giving us time to stretch our legs, and prepare for the next part of our journey which, I for one, was certainly not looking forward to.

A six-hour flight on the back of 'Fat Albert', a C-130 cargo plane, was not something that I particularly relished the thought of. The cavernous hold of the C-130 normally reeked of burning oil and aviation turbine fuel (Avtur) fumes, quickly inducing air-sickness into even the most seasoned of passengers. The thunderous roar of the four turboprop engines reverberated through the cabin, making any sort of conversation impossible, and the thin canvas seats on metal frames could be described as, just about anything, other than comfortable. The in-flight catering usually consisted of a small box containing a couple of curled up ham sandwiches, a packet of ready salted crisps and a lump of cheese. The only toilet facility on board was a large bucket strapped to the fuselage and hidden behind a small curtain.

Whilst joking with Ben about my trousers having more ballroom than Blackpool Tower, a young female RAF Corporal approached us. "We are all ready to go, sir if you are," she said, to none of us in particular.

Daniel, the captain, looked at me and then across at Ben with eyebrows raised, as if to ask us the question.

"SatCom's working fine so let's get on board," chirped up Ben, as he closed the suitcase lid.

In line-astern, we followed the Corporal, who surprised us by walking straight past 'Fat Albert', parked on dispersal, and directly towards a Hawker Siddeley 125 jet. The HS-125 was rarely used for transporting hairy-arsed squaddies such as us, and would normally be reserved for the likes of the prime minister or members of the royal family.

'Sheer luxury!' I thought, as we sat back in the sumptuous leather seats, and were served pre-dinner canapés and champagne in cut-glass flutes.

Whilst flying over the Mediterranean we were receiving confusing messages from the pilots regarding the whereabouts of the hijacked aircraft. Apparently, it had taken off from Beirut and was now sitting in Algiers.

Unable to divert to Algiers, due to a shortage of fuel, we continued towards Akrotiri and agreed that we should decide on our next course of action once we were on the ground.

After landing we were marshalled towards a corner of the Airbase which had been commandeered by, what looked like, half of the American army. A large number of Delta Force were on the ground with civilianised and military vehicles, supported by several fixed-wing and rotary wing aircraft.

A lot had happened whilst we were enjoying living in the lap-of-luxury in Mrs Thatcher's private jet.

After being forced to land in Lebanon by a terrorist holding a hand-grenade with the pin removed in one hand, and a pistol in the other, the passengers and crew then went through a terrifying ordeal, being convinced that the aircraft was about to be blown up. Over the next few hours, the 727 was prepared for flight, and nineteen of the hostages were released in exchange for the aircraft being refuelled.

It then took off and flew to Algeria, where it landed and remained on the ground for about five hours. After that time a further twenty hostages were allowed to leave, and the aircraft returned to Beirut.

On board the hijacked plane the tension was building. All the passengers' passports were collected and everyone with a Jewish-sounding name was segregated from the main body. One young man who produced a US Military passport was dragged from his seat. He was ruthlessly kicked and beaten as he lay in the aisle and hauled towards an exit. The battered and bloodied young sailor was then shot in the head and thrown out onto the ground where another bullet was then fired into his body.

We had an enormous problem on our hands. The normal procedure for establishing an Immediate Action drill as soon as possible, to attempt to save the lives of the hostages, in the event of a rapid deterioration of the situation would, almost certainly, end in a bloodbath.

Beirut Airport was unusual by any standards. At that time Lebanon was engaged in a chaotic and brutal civil war. The airfield had no security fence, and groups of armed militia roamed freely amongst the parked aircraft. Any member of the public could simply walk, or drive, straight onto the active runway, or any other part of the airport for that matter.

The chances of a Deliberate Action, one that is practised and rehearsed, being carried out successfully were almost non-existent. Getting troops on to the ground and close enough to the aircraft to have any effect, could only be achieved after an almost inevitable gunfight. Any exchange of fire close to the hijacked plane was likely to result in, at the very least, the loss of the element of surprise, thereby giving the terrorists plenty of time to carry out their threats and start killing the hostages.

Just as the team were considering and discussing the possible options, intelligence reports indicated that a further group, of at least ten heavily-armed men, had boarded the aircraft. Shortly afterwards, the 727 began to taxi towards the runway as if to prepare for take-off. Our problems had, by then, increased by at least tenfold.

By moving the aircraft, yet again, the terrorists were now making the task of rescuing the hostages almost an impossibility.

We were ordered to prepare to move and, when ready, board the C-5 Galaxy, which was being prepared to follow the peregrinating jetliner, with over a hundred hostages and, at least, twelve extremely dangerous gunmen in control.

CHAPTER THIRTY-TWO

The Lockheed C-5 Galaxy was one of the largest aircraft in the world, dwarfing the British-operated C-130 Hercules. It could carry an enormous payload, which might include vehicles, helicopters and even heavily armoured tanks. With four powerful jet engines, it could fly at the same altitude and speed as a passenger jet and had a useful range of well over two thousand miles.

By the time the massive cargo doors had closed and we were climbing away from Cyprus, we were at least three hours behind the 727, which we were told was about to land, once again, in Algiers. Our Flight Crew received orders to land in Cagliari, on the island of Sardinia, take on fuel, and await further instructions.

In Algiers, the 727 remained on the ground overnight, during which time a further seventy hostages, including the five, female cabin crew, were released. The next morning the aircraft was refuelled and prepared to take-off, but no indication was given as to where it might be heading. Once airborne it climbed out over the Mediterranean, and turned right ninety degrees, generally back towards the Middle East.

We were airborne, in the C-5 Galaxy, as the stricken passenger jet passed in front of us. The pilot identified the 7500 hijack-code transmitted by the aircraft's transponder and tucked in behind it. As the sun began to pass below the horizon behind us, we sat in the 727's contrail and waited to see whereabouts in the troubled Middle East we were about to be lead.

On board the TWA Flight 847, the gang of armed men were clearly in total control of the aircraft. Before take-off one of the gunmen, known as Fajez, who appeared to have some knowledge of aviation and the general layout of the cockpit, had refused to allow the crew to speak on the radio. He had demanded that all communication with the Control Tower was done by him and that only Arabic was spoken rather than English, which is normally adopted anywhere in the world over Air Traffic Control networks

Captain Testrake had been forced to simply follow the instructions given to him, such as – "Take off"; "Climb to cruise altitude"; "Turn to head east". Fajez spoke good English and the captain obeyed.

Only when they were established in the cruise, did the lead terrorist tell the crew what the hostage takers' intentions were. "Now go to Sana'a," he said, pressing the gun against the captain's temple.

All three of the crew shook their heads and objected vociferously, explaining that that was impossible, since they were not carrying any charts for Yemen.

After a short, mumbled discussion between three or four of the hijackers, Fajez spoke again. "Tehran. We will go now to Tehran," emphasising the end of his statement with a pistol-whip to the flight engineer's head.

So, the course was set. Back, more or less, the way they had come. But this time the plan was to fly just to the south of our FOB, then almost directly overhead Beirut, and on to a corner of the world where Americans, and anyone with a Jewish sounding name, would be likely to be made far less than welcome.

By this time the flight engineer, Benjamin Zimmerman, was starting to become thoroughly pissed-off with being beaten about the head with a pistol. He decided that there was no way they were going to land in Iran. He had a plan. A plan that was audacious and dangerous.

Any discussion between the crew members was invariably met with violence. Usually in the form of a crack from a pistol and, more often than not, aimed at poor old Zimmerman who just happened to be sat nearest to the gunman standing guard.

The flight engineer decided that their best option was to land, once again, at Beirut, and this time make sure that they would stay there. He fed Fayez and some of the other English-speaking gang members the line that he was becoming increasingly concerned about the airworthiness of the ageing 727. "The constant flying over the past few days and the lack of any maintenance were beginning to affect the overall performance of the aircraft," he told them with the most concerned look that he could muster. He explained that he was very worried that a major failure was imminent and that he needed to cover the emergency procedures with everyone in case a ditching into the Mediterranean became necessary. He then went into great detail about how to deploy the flimsy and, often unreliable, life-rafts and how important it was to always have shark-repellent close to hand since, in the dark, they would be very unlikely to be rescued and there was no guarantee that the dinghies would stay afloat for long. Zimmerman discreetly threw a couple of switches which lead to gauges reading zero and pointed to them, to emphasise the fact that things were already starting to go wrong. The hostage-takers were now sufficiently convinced that their lives were in impending danger.

As they were approaching the overhead of Beirut the captain called the Control Tower and told them that, due to technical problems, they would have to land there.

"The airport is closed. How much fuel do you have?" asked the controller.

"Maximum flying time of five minutes," lied Captain Testrake.

"It is impossible for you to land. The runway is blocked with vehicles," came the response.

As they started to commence a descent the flight engineer took bold action. He closed-off the fuel supply to the number two engine.

A few seconds later the engine stopped. There then ensued a period of, somewhat overexaggerated, pandemonium on the flight deck, with warning bells and hooters going off, and red lights flashing everywhere. The crew reacted with admirable histrionics, arms flailing about, in typical pilot fashion, and the captain declared a full life-threatening emergency.

Now they did have to land – vehicles or no vehicles.

As the disabled 727 turned on to final approach the crew could clearly see people on the ground frantically trying to get the vehicles cleared from the runway.

With just a few hundred feet to go, Flight Engineer Zimmerman now went completely for broke – he closed the main fuel switch for one of the two remaining engines, knowing that, in a matter of seconds, the engine would stop and they would be unable to stay airborne.

As the wheels touched the runway the engine flamed-out and the aircraft came to a halt.

It was not difficult for the crew to convince everyone that it would now be impossible for them to get off the ground again. All they could do now was await their fate.

As soon as it became clear that Flight TWA 847 was about to land, or perhaps crash, into Beirut Airport, we broke off from the follow and landed at RAF Akrotiri.

As we disembarked from the C-5 Galaxy we were called into a, hastily convened, briefing. We were told that intelligence reports indicated that the hijacked aircraft was very unlikely to go walkabout again. There were still a substantial number of passengers, estimated to about forty, plus the three flight-deck crew, whose lives were in imminent danger. We had to get troops on the ground, close enough to the aircraft to be able to take effective action as quickly as possible.

CHAPTER THIRTY-THREE

I was nominated to become part of a six-man team from Delta Force, who would be flown immediately into northern Israel. (When I say, I was part of a six-man team – I wasn't really. I was being sent forward to fly the plane back to safety if the opportunity arose. The five Delta Force guys were coming along to make sure I didn't get lost, or get taken hostage myself, and to help me to get on board the 727 in one piece.) So I, and my five chaperones, were to be delivered, by helicopter, to a rendezvous point on the Mediterranean coast, north of the town of Nahariyya. Once on the ground, we would be met by agents who would then drive us, the fifty miles or so along the coast, to the airport in Beirut.

We were handed a variety of *shemaghs* and told to dress in the style of the local militia. A style which came very easily to me. I had never been known to be the smartest soldier on parade, and my recently acquired baggy jeans fitted the bill perfectly.

We clambered on board the UH-60 Blackhawk helicopter flown by Warrant Officer Bill Flannery who, coincidentally, had taught me to fly the UH-60 back in 1981 – I knew we were in safe hands.

The six of us huddled together in the back of the Blackhawk in total darkness. A type of darkness rarely experienced. The only source of light ever used during a covert insertion, such as this, was infrared, invisible to the human eye. Wearing ear-defenders to deaden most of the sound and, with absolutely no light whatsoever, I had a feeling of complete disorientation, I had to remind myself that I was hurtling across the sea at high speed and low altitude – less than one hundred feet above the surface. But my senses told me that I could, just as easily, have been floating in space.

I felt Bill reduce the pitch on the blades and raise the nose of the aircraft as we slowed down ready to land. The instant we touched down the side door flew open. The six of us leapt out and crouched on the ground, pulling our *shemaghs* tightly around our heads for protection, as the helicopter climbed away, and the force of the down-wash increased, pressing us into the earth.

Within five seconds the maelstrom subsided, and the sound of the Blackhawk on its way back to Cyprus gradually faded away.

We were met by two agents, also dressed in the typical fashion of the average Lebanese militia member, and led towards a road. Inside each of the two four-by-four Toyotas, parked to one side, were four AK-47 Kalashnikov rifles and one RPG-7 grenade launcher. We were told that the weaponry was primarily to be used as props to complete our disguises. Overtly displaying them in and around the capital should guarantee us safe passage since vehicles carrying heavily armed mobsters were rarely stopped at the numerous roadside checkpoints throughout Lebanon. There was, of course, plenty of ammunition on board just in case we should need it.

We split into two groups, three of us in each four-by-four vehicle.

"My name is Arif," said our driver-cum-agent-cum-guardian. "If we are stopped at any time then please allow me to do the talking."

No argument about that, from me or any of my new colonial buddies.

"Feel free to wave the rifles about as much as you like, especially in built-up areas, but do keep them pointing skywards," said Arif. "Levelling the weapons when other militiamen are around is very likely to result in a firefight, which is not what we are looking for tonight."

As he took his place behind the wheel he patted the glove compartment.

"We have secure covert comms back to headquarters, so we can call up for support if we feel we need it, but I'm hoping that that won't be necessary."

I sat in the back, behind the Israeli Agent and, after checking my rifle for safety, snapped on the thirty-round magazine.

"My job is to get you as close as possible to the hijacked 727, keep it under observation and await further orders," continued Arif as he started the engine. "Sit back and enjoy the ride guys. There is water and something to eat behind the seat."

As we began to pull away the headlights of the other vehicle closed in behind us. Even at that distance, some fifty miles or so, we could make out the loom from war-torn Beirut ahead of us.

My travelling companion was Chuck, who had served in the US Marine Corps before joining Delta Force four years previously. He had completed a short secondment to Hereford in 1982 but, for some reason, our paths had never crossed. Probably down to everyone, at that time, being preoccupied with the war in the Falklands.

Chuck, a dyed-in-the-wool Virginian, took the lead in the vehicle to cover our 'Actions on'. In other words, he ran through what actions we should take in the event that we should come under attack and have to resort to fighting mode. After insisting that we all keep our weapons 'ready' at all times, he then went on to tell me why he was so pleased to be in the Lebanon for the first time. Neither he nor any of the other Americans with us had set foot in this part of the world before. Nevertheless, they were all adamant that their visit was long overdue and they were keen to settle some old scores if they were given half a chance.

Just a few months after the Iraqi and French embassies in Beirut had been destroyed by suicide-car bombers simply driving up to fronts of the buildings and detonating their bombs. A large black van was allowed to approach the front of the US Embassy, despite the guards having been instructed to direct all vehicles to the rear of the building. When it pulled to a halt and exploded the whole central façade of the eight-story building collapsed. Sixty-three people were killed in the bombing and as many as one hundred more were wounded.

Members of the 1st Battalion 8th Marine Corps stationed in Beirut were outraged. More importantly, they were frustrated by their inability to be able to take any sort of constructive action against Hezbollah, the group responsible for the spate of suicide bombings across the city. They felt as though their 'hands were tied' due to the fact, that they had been ordered to operate under Peacetime Rules of Engagement. The effect of the order meant that the Marines were deployed as 'Peacekeepers' and therefore were only allowed to use the absolute minimum of force. When guarding a facility or on patrol they were not allowed to have their weapons 'ready'. A weapon is only ready to use when a magazine containing ammunition is loaded onto it and the weapon is 'cocked' to place a round into the chamber. The only action then required to fire the weapon is to flick off the safety-catch with the thumb and pull the trigger. A sequence which would normally take less than a second.

Less than six months after the murderous assault on the U.S. Embassy a twenty-tonne, yellow Mercedes truck approached the Marine Corps headquarters, close to the International Airport in Beirut. The driver of the truck smiled and waved at the sentries as he approached them before accelerating through the flimsy barrier of barbed wire. Ignoring the order that the guards must not make their weapons 'ready' unless they were given a direct order from a commissioned officer, they made a desperate attempt to cock their weapons and take out the driver, but they simply didn't have enough time to react.

The truck, containing nine tonnes of high explosives, smashed into the entrance-hall of the four-story building and the bomb was detonated. The enormous explosion lifted the entire structure into the air and then collapsed into itself, crushing to death two hundred and forty-one members of the United States Marine Corps. Shortly after the incident, all American forces were withdrawn from the Lebanon.

I was left in no doubt as to why Chuck insisted upon us keeping our weapons 'ready' at all times. I could also see why the guys from the Delta Force headquarters in North Carolina were glad to be back and would not be restricted to the minimum force of peacekeepers if, or more likely when, contact with Hezbollah was made.

A mile or so short of the entrance to the airport both vehicles pulled off the road, and onto a track leading up a hill towards a small wood. We parked by the edge of the wood from where we were clearly able to distinguish the red and white livery of the hijacked TWA jet. With the tree line acting as a backdrop, to prevent us from being sky-lined, someone suggested that we were in a good position to establish an OP. An OP, or Observation Post, is an old military term used to describe any position from where a target can be kept under constant surveillance. It can consist of a solitary individual standing by a lamppost for just a few seconds, or a complex system of tunnels hiding a large number of troops keeping a target under observation for weeks, or even months on end, and can be completely overt or covert. The essential requirement of any OP is that anyone manning it must keep eyes on the target at all times. 'Sod's Law' quite clearly states that, 'The second that you take your eyes off the target something will happen'.

Without knowing how long we might have to man the OP for, we split into two shifts – one car would cover responsibility for four hours while the other car rested. Each occupant of the car on duty would keep their eyes on the target for an hour at a time, whilst the remaining three would keep watch for anyone approaching our position. Keeping one's eyes glued to a target for an hour, especially when using a 'Starlight Scope' at night, is long enough for most individuals to endure.

It was dark and during the very early hours of the morning, while I was dozing in the back of the vehicle, when Randy, a redneck Texan, as he described himself, who had eyes on the target at the time, broke the silence.

"Standby. Standby," he said. "Vehicles approaching the aircraft steps."

We all gathered round and strained our eyes to see exactly what was happening.

The hostages appeared to be being released. They were being lead down the steps and into the awaiting vehicles.

"Let's get down there and follow them," said Chuck.

"Ok, but I need to get authorisation from headquarters first," said our Israeli minder Arif.

"Fuck headquarters. If we don't get down there now we will lose them," retorted Chuck.

Two or three of us shouted our support for Chuck and, without hesitation, we all piled into the vehicles and tore down the hill towards the airport.

We kept our headlights on and played thumping rock music on the radio as we pulled off the main highway and onto the airport approach road. Gangs of militia in this part of the world had a tendency to make their presence felt, so we did the same.

Chuck and I held our Kalashnikov rifles out of the windows and Randy, who was built like a brick shithouse, waved the RPG-7 rocket-launcher, weighing more than twenty pounds, effortlessly in one hand. Not something that I would have been able to do for more than a few seconds.

As a young soldier, I had been made to endure 'Pokey Drill' – not the sort of pastime that someone of my physique and stature was particularly good at. During my basic military training, a whole bunch of us, fledgling squadies, would be lined up in front of the drill sergeant and ordered to follow his actions. He would then hold the standard-issue SLR rifle, which weighed about nine pounds, in his one outstretched arm and wait to see which one of us would crack first. After only a few seconds my muscles would begin to burn and I was invariably one of the first in the squad to lower my arm, and then be punished by having to double around the parade square with my rifle held above my head. No matter how painful my arms might become I would never drop my weapon. Dropping a piece of Her Majesty's equipment, due to utter carelessness, was an almost unspeakable crime, the punishment for which just didn't bear thinking about.

A number of vehicles, with headlights glaring, came towards us – away from the hijacked 727. The first was a technical which was fitted with what appeared to be a Dashka Heavy Machine Gun manned by two turban-clad members of Hezbollah. There then followed a bus and at least three other cars with more technicals bringing up the rear. This had to be the convoy transporting the passengers away from the airport.

"Tuck in behind them," said Chuck, who seemed to have emerged as the leader of our group. "And be prepared to fight."

As Arif moved his hand from the steering wheel and towards the discreet Radio Transmit Button. Chuck reminded him.

"No transmitting this close to the enemy. We are now right next to the building where hundreds of United States Marines were blown to pieces, not long ago, by these bastards in front of us. If things turn nasty then, believe me, I intend to send as many of them to their maker as I possibly can."

The next few seconds would be crucial. If our charade of pretending to be a bunch of drugged-up hoodlums worked, then we would stick with the procession. If not, then Bruce Springsteen, who was by then hammering our eardrums with his latest rock song, was not the only one who was going to be 'On Fire'.

CHAPTER THIRTY-FOUR

Our ruse appeared to be working as we were allowed to join the procession, unmolested, towards the centre of Beirut. Other vehicles soon drew up behind us which we had to assume were carrying more well-armed members of Hezbollah, and therefore to be regarded as enemy. We now felt that we had enemy to our front and rear, and if we were to be exposed at this stage then the ensuing firefight was likely to be completely chaotic and bloody. We all remained extremely tense and on edge as we approached, what appeared to be, a major roadside checkpoint on the southern outskirts of the city. Bright lights were trained on to the approaching vehicles and a number of armed militiamen stood either side of the road checking each vehicle in turn.

An acrid, almost metallic, taste of fear welled up in the back of my throat and I felt a sudden urge to leap out of the car and run towards the safety of the shadows, but I managed to keep it under control.

"Hold fast guys," whispered Chuck as Arif turned off the radio. "We have no option now other than to stick with it. Keep your weapons ready but pointed skywards."

We slowly drove into the pool of light at the checkpoint as the bus, and the cars in front of us were waved through without being stopped. The first of the technicals was then allowed to pass after a very brief exchange of words and was quickly followed by the second. We came to a halt a few metres in front of the lights and the ominous-looking heavy machine-guns pointing directly at us, as a gunman walked towards us.

"*As-salam Alaikum*," shouted Arif, as the gunman stopped in front of us.

As the Arab opened his mouth to reply there was a shout from the area of the parked vehicles and he suddenly turned and ran back towards them.

"Standby," said Chuck, as calmly as if he were about to order a Big Mac and fries from his local MacDonald's. "On my command, Randy, you take the gun on the left with the RPG. Red, you and I will take the one on the right. Arif, you get ready to drive like fuck out of here! Hold fire for now."

I waited, with my heart pounding in my chest, ready to flick the safety-catch with my thumb past the first detent, for single-shots and through to the second for fully-automatic, and let rip with a full magazine towards the back of the machine gun. But, things didn't develop quite as we were expecting them to.

The dazzling lights of the checkpoint were switched off and the machine guns began to turn away from us, as the gunmen loaded onto the technical and started to move off after the motorcade.

We sat in utter disbelief as we realised that, instead of having to fight for our lives, we were, once again, joining the convoy of hostages and hijackers.

"Well, fuck my old boots," said Randy with a beaming smile. "Looks like we are back on the waggon train."

Just as we entered the busy streets of the city and caught up with the vehicles ahead of us, the column split into three. Two cars and one technical turned right, and another car and a second technical turned left and disappeared down narrow side roads. The bus and the remaining vehicles carried straight on

"Stick with the bus," ordered Chuck as he waved to the car behind us to follow on. Just then the vehicle directly in front of us came to a halt, blocking the way, as the bus, with the majority of the hostages on board, disappeared into the bustling side roads of southern Beirut.

We were desperate to find where the hostages were going to be housed, but despite driving like blue-arsed flies, around the area where the convoy was last seen, for at least a couple of hours, we found nothing. We couldn't even give any reasonable estimate of where they might then be being imprisoned, in order for a rescue mission to be launched. I am sure we all felt deflated and demoralised but we had to report the situation to our headquarters – a Sitrep as it was known to us. Just before dawn we were ordered to return to the helicopter drop-off point in Israel to be picked up and returned to the FOB in Cyprus.

About two weeks after our return the hostages were released, unharmed, from a number of different locations across the southern suburbs of Beirut, after more than seven hundred Shiite prisoners were freed from Israeli jails, thereby meeting the initial demands of the hostage-takers. The United States Government, however, steadfastly denied that they had given in to the terrorists, claiming that they had secured the release of all the hostages only by clever diplomatic negotiations. It was, they insisted, pure coincidence that the hijackers had demanded that seven hundred prisoners be released from Israel, and that, just before they arranged the release of the hostages a very similar number just happened to be allowed to leave Israeli jails

CHAPTER THIRTY-FIVE
SILVER MOUNTAIN

"Right leg or left leg?"

"I prefer right."

"Well so do I."

"Look. We can't both go for right – unless you want to go around in fucking circles for the next six days."

"Ok. Ok. Let's toss for it then. His Excellency is getting really pissed off."

The conversation, which I admit, might sound a bit weird, was between Don Craven and myself. We were arguing over which legs we should strap together before attempting to climb Mount Kilimanjaro 'three-legged'. The British High Commissioner from the consulate in Dar es Salaam was present, and waiting to seal the bonds with his official 'waxy thingamajig'.

We planned to meet six days later, after returning from the peak, when he would then confirm that the seal had not been broken to authenticate that the charity stunt had been completed successfully.

Don and I were both serving members of the Army Air Corps at the time. We had done some climbing together in the Italian Alps and the High Atlas Mountains in Morocco. Neither of us was, what you might call, an accomplished mountaineer. It was more a case of us wanting to get away for a couple of weeks each year without having to pay for a package holiday. Adventurous training was, very much, encouraged in the British Army. Organising expeditions and taking younger soldiers on such trips was a good way to do it at Her Majesty's expense. It was 1982 and, although life was far from dull. we still felt that we needed some sort of wheeze to get away to somewhere interesting for a fortnight or so.

That year was the Silver Jubilee Year of the Army Air Corps and between us, we hatched a plot.

To coincide with the silver jubilee year why not climb the 'Silver Mountain', the name given to Mount Kilimanjaro in East Africa? And why not climb it to raise money for charity? And, while we were at it, why not attempt to set a world record by climbing it 'three-legged'?

"What a great idea," we both agreed. "Don't suppose, for one minute, that the top brass will fall for it, but let's give it a try anyway."

We put the proposal together and sent it to the Ministry of Defence via our regimental headquarters, not expecting, for one minute, that it would be accepted.

A few weeks later, much to our surprise, our proposal was officially sanctioned, and Exercise Silver Mountain was up and running.

I won the toss. We strapped our legs together, my right with Don's left.

His Excellency applied the official seal of Her Britannic Majesty's representative in Tanzania, looked at us as if we were completely bonkers, and left us at the base of the mountain. The starting point was just outside Moshi were we all agreed to meet, after the climb, for the High Commissioner to confirm that the seal was still intact.

Don and I had reached the peak of the mountain a few weeks previously, on a recce, so we knew what to expect.

Kilimanjaro is a cat's whisker short of twenty thousand feet high. A dormant volcano, rising up from the Serengeti Plain in northern Tanzania, it was first climbed by Doctor Hans Meyer in 1889 and it was long disbelieved that snow could remain without melting, so close to the equator. Not only is Mount Kilimanjaro permanently covered in snow, but the icecap is no less than two hundred feet thick. The route to the top of the volcano, Uhuru Peak, cannot be described as a 'technical climb' in mountaineering terms. It is a walk, with a bit of a scramble up the final two thousand feet or so.

The main stumbling block with an ascent such as the one we were about to undertake, was likely to be altitude sickness. Neither of us had suffered much from it on any previous climbs so we felt pretty relaxed, and didn't expect to encounter any real problems.

Our main concern was rather more basic. We were going to be tethered to one and other for six days. We had to eat and drink – the consequences of which were inevitable. Anything more serious than a pee stop was not something we looked forward to, but it was something we had thought about, at great length, and prepared for in true military fashion.

There was a procedure which we had put in place which had to be adhered to. Once one of us became aware that the need for a 'comfort break' was becoming necessary, we would call out two numbers. Unless just a pee was needed the first would always be 'two'. The second would progress from 'one' to 'six' depending on the level of desperation. For example, 'Two one', spoken in a, gently modulated, and controlled voice, meant that there was no immediate urgency, and we had plenty of time to carry out the well-rehearsed routine.

'Two six', uttered in a high-pitched squeal, however, meant that the situation was critical and was not something either of us was looking forward to hearing.

Upon receipt of the coded message, and depending upon the magnitude of the second digit we would break off from the well-trodden path and endeavour to find a reasonably flat piece of ground. (Not always the easiest of things to find on the side of a mountain.) Coping with a steep slope was something we never really came to terms with or even agreed upon an ideal strategy. Was the best manoeuvre to face uphill, downhill, or athwartships? The question seemed to be unfathomable. The potential for a mishap on anything steeper than a one-in-five gradient was enormous. Throw in the fact that we might be dealing with a 'two four', or even a 'two six', and the outcome had the potential to be disastrous.

Once a reasonably level area of the mountainside had been identified, the next thing to do was to wet the first finger of one's right hand, stick it up in the air, and assess the direction of the wind. Whichever one of us was not in need would then face into the prevailing wind, lie on the ground, and bury their face, as far into the earth, as they could bear. Ramming fingers into each ear and singing 'La, La, La' at the top of their voice was an alternative to eating dirt, but this was left entirely to the individual's discretion.

At night, we would sleep, intermittently, on the floor of one of the huts provided by the National Park Authority rather than share one of the small bunk beds.

We completed the climb successfully and arrived back at the rendezvous point, outside Moshi, at the agreed time, eager to get our bonds released. After waiting for more than an hour for the high commissioner, we realised that we had been stood up. Not wanting to spend any more time strapped together than we had to, we asked the chief ranger to issue us with a certificate stating that we had successfully completed the climb 'three-legged'. Which, thankfully, he agreed to, for a small price, of course. We released the strap which had bound us together for more than six days, swearing never to come within a yard of each other ever again.

We raised almost twenty thousand pounds for our chosen charities. Giving ten thousand to the Rockfield Centre for the Mentally Handicapped in Hereford for them to build a new classroom, and the remainder of the money we donated to the Army Air Corps Benevolent Fund. We left a plaque engraved with details of the climb secured to a rock on the peak and, so far as I am aware, it is still there. Whether or not the event was ever recorded as a world record was of little consequence to us. We had raised a substantial amount of money for charity and had a whole load of laughs along the way. So, as far as we were concerned, the object of the exercise had certainly been achieved.

CHAPTER THIRTY-SIX
SIERRA LEONE

In 1994 I was married for the second time, and living in a converted barn on the edge of the West Pennine Moor in Lancashire. Not quite retired, but my employment with MI6 was not full-time, which meant that I had plenty of free time away from the rigours of flying and spying.

Life was good, and I could afford to spend, not only time but also money, on improving my pleasant rural retreat, with its lake and six acres of land.

As I was putting the finishing touches to the dry-stone wall, which I had built along the edge of the lake, and, of which I was immensely proud, my phone rang. (To be honest, I didn't have a lake – it was more of a pond, and not a very big one, at that.)

It was a long-term friend of mine from our days in the SAS, and, more recently, our involvement with Sir David Sterling's Private Security Company KAS, which he ran from his offices in 22 South Audley Street in Mayfair. (I never did deduce whether Sir David having his offices in 22 South Audley Street – 22 SAS – was by accident or design.)

My long-term friend explained that he was involved in a couple of projects in West Africa and wondered if I might like to get involved.

"Could be very interesting, and exciting for you Red," he said with a chuckle. "And you will be working with our old mate Fred, so it's bound to be fun."

When mixed together, the cocktail of the words interesting, exciting, fun. West Africa and, most of all, Fred, had the potential to lead to a perilous situation, especially when coming from the mouth of one such as Simon Mann, better known to me as 'Captain Chaos'.

Ten years previously Simon had worked with Fred and me when we had first left the Army, and started the company KAS, with Sir David Stirling as chairman and Colonel Ian Crook as the managing director.

In the company offices in Mayfair, we would often sit around the fire in the boardroom, conspiring about KAS's future, and working out ways of making money for the fledgling business. I was certainly no accountant, but it seemed to me that most of the company funds were being spent on – vodka for the chairman; Sancerre, for the managing director; and expensive cigars, which they both smoked incessantly. David was insistent that alcohol and tobacco were not luxuries, but were essential for the smooth running of the company, and were, therefore, perfectly legitimate business expenses.

Shortly after KAS was formed, Sir David, Crookie and myself went on a trip to the United States in an attempt to drum up some much-needed, business. Whilst staying in the capital we met with President Reagan, and then had lunch with George Bush and the deputy director of the secret service, Bob de Prospero, in the White House. Just across the road from the White House was the Hay Adams Hotel, then the most prestigious, and expensive in Washington, and of course, at the chairman's insistence, that is where we had to stay.

With such huge outgoings and very little income, the company was doomed, and it wasn't long before KAS was wound up.

Working so closely with the legendary founder of the SAS had been a great privilege. His eccentricity and roguish sense of humour had made it tremendous fun, and it was a sad day indeed when we packed up and left South Audley Street for the last time. As a farewell present Sir David Stirling DSO, OBE, gave me his old desk, which he had brought down from his family's estate in Scotland, and a photocopying machine, to help me get started in business. The desk I still have, and cherish. The photocopier has long since been disposed of.

I caught the West Coast train from Preston to London Euston and from there continued on the Tube to Sloane Square. Seeing as it was such a pleasant spring day I decided to walk the length of the Kings Road to the offices of Branch Energy, which was then run by Tony Buckingham.

Tony, Simon and I sat around the boardroom table for our meeting.

It came as something of a surprise when I was asked, without undue ceremony, if I would like to help, in some way, with the fight against the rebels in Sierra Leone.

Sierra Leone, on the west coast of Africa, with its capital Freetown was, until 1961 a British colony, and then one of the wealthiest countries on the continent. In recent years, it had been reduced to a shambles and a civil war broke out in 1990. Valentine Strasser, an ex-captain in the Army, and now the country's incumbent president, had risen to power after staging a military coup in 1992.

A drug-fuelled rebel group known as the RUF was reigning terror throughout the villages and towns of the country's interior, inflicting almost unspeakable atrocities on the population.

Villages were raided indiscriminately. Women and children were raped and tortured. Often whole families were herded into their huts and burned to death. One of the RUF's trademarks and sources of amusement was to ask a terrified victim if he, or she, preferred to wear long or short sleeves, before hacking off their arms at the wrist or elbow.

Large, natural sources of mineral wealth, existed in the country, such as rutile and bauxite. But the commodity that aroused the most interest to those inside, and outside, of the country was diamonds.

Executive Outcomes (EO), a private military company, based in South Africa, in which Tony and Simon had some interest, was becoming established in Sierra Leone to support the government in its struggle against the RUF.

It was proposed that, once in the theatre, I would work alongside Fred, who was already based in a suburb of Freetown. Fred and I would be required to come under the command and control of EO. This was a loose arrangement, which was necessary due to the dangerous environment existing for any expatriates, or foreigners, operating just about anywhere, in the country at that time. Working under EO's umbrella would mean that we would be able to call on them to get us out of the shit, should the need ever arise.

It didn't take long for the need to arise. Shortly after starting our operation Fred and I were desperately in need of the South Africans, with their helicopters, and their military expertise.

CHAPTER THIRTY-SEVEN

After leaving London and transiting through Schiphol in the Netherlands I arrived in Lungi, the nation's only airport, about ten miles north of Freetown. First impressions were not good. The terminal buildings and hangars were in dire need of a lick of paint. The grassed areas were overgrown, tumble-weed blew across the taxiways, and a few, tatty-looking old Russian air-craft littered the dispersal areas. The only two aircraft that looked at least half-decent were the ones in white livery with large black 'UN' insignia emblazoned on each tail-fin. It's a fairly safe bet that, in any country in the world that is ravaged by war or starvation, the toothless and, in my opinion, ineffectual, United Nations will invariably be found. Their personnel safely tucked away in a heavily fortified UN compound or, driving around in their top-of-the-range, air-conditioned bulletproof Land Cruisers. Again, in my humble opinion, the UN soldiers have become the world's past masters at 'standing by and watching what's going on'.

As I stepped off the plane into the oppressive West African heat, I was met, at the bottom of the steps by my old friend Fred.

"Welcome brother," he said, almost lifting me off the ground in a bear hug.

Fred was a larger-than-life, ex-SAS warrant officer, who hailed from the Fijian, South Pacific island of Rotuma. He was known to be fiercely loyal and honest, and wanted passionately to help the subjugated and terrorised people of this war-torn country. Not because he was scheming to capitalise further down the line if peace ever came. But he was, quite simply, a decent and caring individual.

I couldn't wait to get into the terminal building, out of the stifling heat of the African sun. But passing through the 'Arrivals' door turned out to be a big disappointment – it was even hotter inside than it was outside. A mass of people was packed into the arrivals hall, pushing and shoving each other, to get to the front of the queues for each of the many counters. Behind each of the counters stood at least one official that had to be dealt with before entry clearance could be granted; baggage collection, customs, immigration, visa payment, visa issue, police and security. Each official, in turn, had to be presented, not only with one's passport, but also a processing fee and, a 'small gratuity'. Without a good elbow action, and a ready supply of ten-dollar bills the whole process could take hours.

But, thankfully, I was spared all that rigmarole. All I did was follow Fred who, in turn, followed a local guy, with a bright yellow jacket and an official-looking ID hung around his neck. We went into an empty, quiet and cool room, off to the side of the main hall, marked 'VIP Lounge', where my passport was processed immediately, and we were on our way – no queues, no bribes.

Although we were only ten miles from the capital the road trip would have taken, not less than five hours, due to the circuitous route, and the almost impassable roads.

We left the air-conditioned environment via a second door, this time displaying the sign 'Helipad – VIPs only', and there, with engines running and rotors turning, stood an ageing, Mi-8 Russian helicopter. Fred gave the 'guide' the very convoluted, and time-consuming 'Leonian' handshake, finishing with the palming across of a twenty-dollar bill, and we jumped on board the helicopter. Within ten minutes of strapping ourselves into the dirty, canvas seats we were on final approach for our landing site at a hotel on the outskirts of Freetown. We were already checked-in to the hotel, which had certainly seen better days, but the receptionist was friendly, and handed us a cool glass of Tusker beer as a welcome, before recommending that we take some further refreshments in the bar before retiring to our rooms.

At the entrance to the restaurant and bar was a sign chalked onto a piece of blackboard, which I loved, but never fully understood.

'Welcome to the MAMMY YOKO HOTEL. No ganja, No pettin, No Bull dancin..

The following morning a Land Rover arrived at the hotel to pick us up.

Fred had already briefed me that we were going to Bo, a small town about one hundred and fifty miles south-east of Freetown, to meet Sam Hinga Norman.

Sam Norman was a paramount chief of the Jaiama Bongor region, and he and Fred were working together to establish a Civil Defence Force, which they had named 'The Kamajor', meaning 'hunter'.

The Kamajor had not got off to a good start. Recently the chief had gathered together seventy-five, young, energetic men to defend his people and, after the first attack by the rebels on his chiefdom, no less than fifty of them, were killed.

Anywhere outside of the environs of the capital, more especially towards Bo, was dangerous. Vehicles, such as the one we would be in, were prone to attack by marauding gangs of the ruthless RUF rebels.

Fred was dressed in 'jungle-greens' combat gear, a khaki bandana, and looking, very much, as if he 'meant business'. I, on the other hand, wore jeans and a T-shirt and was unlikely to deter even a schoolboy mugger.

We discussed our 'actions-on', in other words, what we would do should we come under attack.

I was handed a nine-millimetre Browning pistol, and two twelve-round magazines of ammunition, which I stuck into my belt. In the footwell behind the driver, there were two AK-47s, both with two magazines containing thirty rounds of 7.62 ammo. Fred pointed out three small rucksacks, which he explained, contained basic survival equipment and water.

"In the event of a contact," ordered Fred, in his ex-sergeant major's voice. 'I will exit left, and you will exit right. Remember Red, we can survive for three weeks without food – three days without water – and three minutes without ammo'. He continued, as he pulled back a tarpaulin and uncovered two, one-thousand round, boxes of 7.62 NATO Ball ammunition.

'Let's go, George my friend', said The Fijian Warrior, pointing as if he were leading a cavalry charge.

The road eastwards, as far as Mile 91, was reasonable, probably equivalent to a badly neglected B-class road in the UK. Thereafter the route could be very rough, depending on how much of the surface had been washed away by the regular tropical storms.

With an hour or so, to run to Bo, Fred said something to George in the local 'Krio' dialect, a form of Pidgin-English native to this part of the world.

We pulled off the road which, by now, had become, not much more than a rough bridle-path, and set off down a much smaller track, through dense jungle. After a short, bumpy ride, we entered a clearing which housed a small village consisting of mud huts with thatched roofs, and the occasional piece of plywood or corrugated-iron sheeting. We stopped and stood by the vehicle, stretching our legs, sipping water and looking around the village, which appeared to be completely deserted.

146

"Is this your idea of a Motorway Services, mate? What the fuck are we doing, miles off the main road, in a deserted jungle village," I asked as I peeled a banana.

"Be patient, Red. The people here are like wounded kittens. They will come out when they are ready."

And slowly, with great caution, they did.

First to emerge from the dense undergrowth was the village elder who, upon recognising Fred, gave a toothless grin and hobbled towards us. They greeted each other like long-lost brothers, hugging and chanting words I didn't understand. The old man was crying. After hearing the stories, the villagers had to tell, I could see why.

CHAPTER THIRTY-EIGHT

A small crowd of villagers gradually gathered around us. One of them was a young woman, who held on to Fred's arm, looking up at him adoringly, as if he were some sort of saviour – in a way I suppose he was. She would, surely, have smiled at him, but that wasn't possible.

Her name was Blossom and she had once been beautiful. Now she looked as though she was wearing some sort of hideous, Halloween face-mask. She was unable to speak. Her top and bottom lips were missing completely, exposing her, perfectly symmetrical, white teeth.

A few months ago, as the men of the village were away fishing and hunting, the women sat around preparing dinner, whilst the children played happily nearby.

Suddenly, deafening shots rang out, and a gang of RUF rebels, some of them as young as twelve, burst into the clearing.

Blossom, with her seven-month-old baby Yaema, strapped to her back, ran into the closest hut and dived under the bed.

Yeama was screaming and the door burst open. Blossom was dragged outside by her hair and made to witness the baying gang getting pleasure from chopping off the right hand of nine-year-old Daniel.

Their attention then turned to the beautiful, young, terrified mother. The bonds on her back were roughly cut away, and her baby was dragged from her. One young rebel held the baby aloft by a leg, and, with one swift slash of his razor-sharp *panga*, disembowelled the wriggling child, much to the amusement of the other young gang members.

Blossom fell to her knees – distraught. As she was held, the end of her tongue was sliced off. A wooden skewer was then driven through her top and bottom lips, and a large padlock clamped into the holes as she was, mockingly, told not to speak to anyone from the government, ever again.

Blossom was one of a dozen villagers left lying in the dirt, bleeding from appalling wounds, with a further ten lying dead.

The ensuing infection from the rusty padlock, left the pitiful young woman with a large section of her face cut away and, as she tried to explain in mime, her heart ripped from her body, over the death of her sweet baby Yaema.

As Fred translated the spoken words of the elder and the sign-language of Blossom, tears streamed down his cheeks.

'Something has to be done to stop this madness' he said, holding Blossom closely to his side.

Now, more than twenty years later, the memory of that gathering in the remote, jungle village overwhelms me with emotion.

CHAPTER THIRTY-NINE

At the meeting with the paramount chief, in his hometown of Bo, we came up with a proposition to help support the embryonic Citizens Defence Force – The Kamajos. Sam made it clear to us that everything in Sierra Leone could be bought, including weapons and training. What he needed, more than anything, was money.

The area around Bo and Kenema was one of the richest sources of diamonds in the world. Most of the diamonds, that were either dredged from the river beds or dug out from the ground, were smuggled out of the country, resulting in no benefit for the government or its citizens.

The local inhabitants, who managed to scratch the diamonds from the earth, either sold them to one of the ubiquitous foreign dealers at a fraction of their true value, or they attempted to smuggle them out of the country where they were likely to get a slightly better price.

Our plan was to buy rough, uncut diamonds, directly from the locals in Kenema. After renting an office in the town centre, we would spread the word that we were willing to pay far better prices than any of the local dealers. We would process the consignment through the appropriate government office and pay any due taxes. I would then deliver it, by hand, to a reputable dealer in Antwerp with whom we would be able to negotiate a fair price. After taking out a small amount to repay the initial investment, plus a return of fifteen percent, any remaining profit would be paid to the Chief to fund the Kamajors.

It certainly seemed to be a good idea, and a fair deal all around. The individuals finding the diamonds would benefit, as would the government, the investors and the much-needed Defence Force.

With that plan in mind, it was decided that I should return to London to get the scheme started. Leaving Fred to deal with the tiresome and bureaucratic process of getting the necessary 'Diamond Dealers Licence'.

It didn't take me long to convince Tony Buckingham and Simon Mann that the concept had 'legs', and with their help, I could get together the one hundred thousand dollars, or so, that was needed to get the project under way.

Since the buying and selling of the diamonds were going to be down to me, we all agreed that the sensible thing for me to do, was to start by learning something about those enigmatic polymorphs of carbon.

I found a dealer by the name of Monsieur Coquoin, who had premises in Hoveniersstraat, Antwerp, who said he would be willing to teach me how to assess the value of rough, uncut diamonds – for a price, of course. I was more than a little surprised to be told that I would need to spend, at least a week with M Coquoin to become, even reasonably proficient – I was thinking, more like a day.

So, spend a week with him is what I did. With French, not being my strong point, I found it easier to refer to my tutor as 'Monsieur Cock', which he seemed to find quite amusing and acceptable.

Ready to set off to Africa in my new role as 'Diamond Evaluator', Monsieur Cock shook my hand and declared that I was now *'competant – a peine'*. He then convinced me that I must buy all the necessary paraphernalia; magnifying loupe, diamond tester, scales, polariscope and lots of other bits and pieces, none of which I was sure how to use.

CHAPTER FORTY

Our ever-reliable and faithful driver George turned up at the Mammy Yoko Hotel, in good time for us to get on the road to Kenema, where we had now rented a small office. The Land Rover was loaded with all the armaments we might need in the event of an attack, plus several bags of flour and rice, which we intended to drop off at Blossom's village on the way past. We also had two extra rucksacks. One containing US dollars – about forty thousand. And the second containing the local currency, Leones. I can't remember how many, but it would certainly have been in the hundreds of thousands.

The office was sparse, just a table and three, or four, chairs. We set out our stall, ready to start trading. I would sit behind the desk, with the bags of money at my feet, surrounded by all the tools-of-the-trade, sold to me by Monsieur Cock. Faithful George sat in the corner opposite me, ready to act as an interpreter if it became necessary.

Fred, looking every inch the Special Forces warrior that he was, stood to my side, a pistol strapped to his waist and his AK-47 slung across his chest, his right hand never straying from the trigger.

As we 'opened for business', we were pleased to see that we already had a queue of six or seven potential clients waiting in the corridor.

Trading went well, and by the time we were due to shut up shop, we had a good stash of diamonds, the veracity of every single one confirmed with the diamond tester, the weight, clarity and colour carefully logged. We had parted with, the best part of thirty thousand dollars – no one had shown the slightest interest in the local currency.

We were now prime targets for an attack. The route back to Freetown offered little opportunity for diverging from the main road. To minimise the likelihood of an ambush we left the office in the opposite direction to the capital. A small track lead us to a clearing on a plateau, and as we came to a halt we heard the familiar rattle of the EO's helicopter. We quickly loaded all our goodies into the back, with the loadmaster and door-gunner training their weapons towards the surrounding jungle.

Juba, one of the Ibis Air pilots, had us safely back on the ground in Freetown in less than an hour. Ibis Air was Simon Mann's aviation company which provided air support for Executive Outcomes.

Soon after I had completed the tedious palaver of getting authority to export our cache and paid the relevant taxes, I was sipping a glass of bubbly in the forward cabin of a 747, on my way back to Antwerp.

Monsieur Cock emptied the bag of diamonds onto his desk and studied each one, as only a true professional could. Whilst looking over his glasses at me, he said in a slow studious voice, "Fifty-two thousand dollars."

"That's a deal," I said with a smile, not even thinking that I should negotiate.

The smile he returned – the largest one I had ever seen him crack, showed me that the mentor was pleased with his apprentice's performance.

After expenses, I reckoned we had cleared a profit of about ten thousand dollars.

The operation was looking good, and the chief was delighted with the twenty thousand smackers I was happy to give him – the extra ten was in anticipation of future successful deals.

Our intention was to repeat the transactions on a regular basis, but we were acutely aware of the dangers of ambush or attack if we were ever to establish any sort of pattern of behaviour.

For our second attempt, we passed a message saying that we would be travelling down to Kenema, by road, on a Friday. However, known only to our three-man procurement team, Fred, George and I, we left our hotel in the early hours of the preceding Wednesday, again dropping supplies off at the isolated village.

Another good haul was gathered and we were in good humour as we left the office. George looked particularly happy as he pocketed his handsome bonus, and volunteered to 'take care of the diamonds'.

We drove off, in an unpredictable direction, towards the planned helicopter pick-up point, totally unaware that we were about to be betrayed, putting our lives in real and imminent danger.

The larger-than-life Fijian was riding shot-gun and munching on a mango as he said cheerfully, "George my friend, I think you are taking us down the wrong track. Leading us up the garden path. As we say in England."

As we approached a sharp bend, George said nothing. A few seconds later, there in front of us, was a barrier with an old police car parked to one side and four men, dressed in scruffy blue uniforms, standing with the ever-present AK-47s, pointed directly towards us.

George stopped immediately and switched off the ignition, as two more armed officers-of-the-law closed in behind us.

Much as it ran against the grain, especially for a seasoned warrior such as Fred, we had no option other than to de-bus and surrender ourselves to our captors, rather than put up a fight.

I breathed a sigh of relief as we were handcuffed. This could only mean that our captors were not members of the barbaric RUF, but were indeed real police. And real police, in this part of the world, could very easily be bought.

'Show me your diamond dealers' licence,' said one of the policemen, who I guessed was the boss, since he was proudly sporting some sort of official-looking badge and wearing LAPD-like shades, held together with some rather alluring, masking tape.

"George," I shouted over my shoulder. "Show him the licence please."

"George… George! Where the fuck is George?"

But faithful old George had gone. As had the diamonds and the licence – never to be seen again.

"Ok mate, just see if you can get the bag out of the Land Rover and give them a wedge of that local money that nobody else wants," I whispered.

"No Red, we have to make a stand against corruption, starting now, if this country is ever going to make any progress," replied an indignant Fred.

"Bollocks to that," I exclaimed, amazed at Fred's morality. "You can give them the whole fucking bag if it makes you feel better, but let's get the fuck out of here."

But no. Fred was a man of principles and there was no way he was going to budge.

We were bundled into the back of the police vehicle as the officers, waving their weapons in the air, cheered and performed a well-rehearsed, victory war-dance, before driving off.

CHAPTER FORTY-ONE

In the British Military, all troops prone to captures, such as Special Forces or aircrew, are required to undergo 'Combat Survival' exercises and 'Resistance to Interrogation' training. It had been pumped into both of us, back in our SAS days, that, when taken prisoner, you must, if at all possible, try to escape. Trying to escape, as soon after capture as possible is considered the best option, while you are still fit, and thereby giving yourself the most likely chance of a successful break for freedom.

As we sat across from each other, handcuffed and feeling sorry for ourselves, in the open-backed truck, we made eye contact, and there was no doubt that each of us knew what the other was thinking.

Our captors had made a rudimentary mistake by handcuffing us with our hands if front of us, and not behind our backs. To either side of the bumpy track was dense, secondary jungle. Secondary jungle is much more overgrown than primary jungle and therefore a lot harder to make progress through, especially without a machete or a *panga*. But it had the distinct advantage of being much easier to hide in.

I hadn't worked on my escape plan in too much detail – in fact, I hadn't given it any thought at all. As the vehicle slowed down slightly I dived, Superman-like over Fred's shoulder and rolled into the surrounding jungle. Hardly able to penetrate the dense undergrowth, I pushed forward for only a few yards before crawling under some low-lying vegetation, burrowed myself into the earth as much as possible, and lay still.

I heard footsteps running towards me and then Fred's voice shouting out, "Go for it mate. See you back at the bar and make mine a flaming Drambuie." Followed by his booming laughter.

The pain in my shoulder was starting to overwhelm me as I lay motionless, hardly daring to breathe. I reckoned that, if I could stay hidden for another hour or so, then, under the cover of darkness, I would have a reasonable chance of making my way back to Bo. Once there, with any luck, I would be able to contact the chief, who I knew would be more than happy to help. My plan was starting to come together nicely.

Fred was still laughing as I was dragged squealing, like a stuffed pig, back towards the vehicle.

"Mate, I could see you from here," he chuckled.

My heroic break for freedom had lasted a full five minutes, and the pain in my shoulder made it too difficult for me to break into a smile, let alone laugh.

The LAPD wannabe was far from happy. He held his pistol to my head and screamed something incomprehensible to me, but I think I got the gist. 'Don't you dare do that again.'

Fred just gave me a sideways glance, with raised eyebrows, and shook his head slowly, as a headmaster might do to a naughty schoolboy.

In later years, he would take great pleasure in taking the piss out of me. Often relating the story of me diving into the dense jungle, burying my head under a few leaves, and sticking my arse up in the air for all to see. Sometimes even comparing my 'great escape' to that of Sir David Sterling's exploits during the Second World War.

The 'basha-up Beatles' were taking to the air as we passed through the shoddily-constructed gate at the entrance to a small compound, surrounded by bamboo fencing and barbed wire.

('Basha-up Beatles' were so called because they tended to get airborne in the jungle just before last light. A timely reminder that it was then time to get one's basha or bed, erected before it got too dark.)

We were lead into a small pitch-black cell. One of our captors lit a candle, exposing windowless walls, two rickety beds and a bucket in one corner.

With a rifle pointing ominously towards us, our handcuffs were removed. Before closing the door, the policeman made a point of making us aware of the armed guard seated just outside.

My roommate was a qualified 'patrol-medic', having passed the course when he was starting his career in the regiment. After checking out my shoulder, by pulling my arm about and putting me through agony for, what seemed like an age, he proudly declared that I was 'fit to fly', and nothing was broken. He then strongly recommended that I get some rest, and save 'the great escape 2' until we had had a chance to see what we were up against in the light of day.

Chuntering and feeling very sorry for myself I took the advice and settled down for a few hours' rest. At some point in the night, a hatch was opened in the door, and a plastic bottle filled with water and a metal dish containing, what looked vaguely like rice, was passed through to us.

At night, the jungle comes alive with noise. From the distant roar of some large predator to the chatter of monkeys, the drone of flying insects, the rustle of creatures crawling around the floor and the constant buzz of mosquitos. And for us, there was the incessant plodding, and sometimes tuneless humming, of the all-too-vigilant sentry.

Shards of light breaking through the numerous cracks in the walls of the flimsily-built prison-cell woke me from a fretful sleep.

Fred was already awake, sitting on his basha, and cleaning his teeth with a small splinter of wood.

The only time we were allowed out of our cell was each morning to empty the bucket into a stinking trench at the far side of the compound, and, even then, one of us had to remain behind. As pathetic as it may seem, that walk across the small enclosure was our only bit of recreation, and we looked forward to it. The morning promenade also gave us the opportunity to scrutinise the fence and identify any possible weak spots.

It didn't take long for our military 'combat survival' training to kick in. In no time at all we had organised an escape committee and, because of my previous experience, I was voted in as chairman. We sat on our bashas facing each other and, on the very first committee meeting, came up with an escape plan. Which I thought was highly commendable.

The first thing we would need was access to the compound, so we started by scraping away at one of the walls. In keeping with the finest traditions of World-War-Two escapees, we masked any excess noise by humming merry tunes, whistling or simply by talking very loudly. Any superfluous scrapings were dumped in the bucket and duly disposed of. In only a few hours we had loosened an area of the wall large enough for Fred to get through, and felt reasonably confident that it would take only a gentle push to provide us with a large enough opening for us to get our break-out underway.

On a chosen night, we would wait until just after midnight and then, carefully, listen to the sentry. If, and when, we could both confirm that the guard was sitting on the chair by the door, then I would try to attract his attention in some way. Not enough to alarm him, but just enough to raise his interest and keep him in that position.

Now, I must admit that the next part of our plan was, somewhat lacking in detail. But it was all we had.

Once through the hole in the wall, Fred would then sneak around, behind the distracted guard, snaffle his rifle, and subdue him whilst I bound and gagged him with the bits of nylon twine gathered from the beds.

That done, the ex-Fijian rugby player would hurtle himself towards the pre-reccied soft spot in the fence, with me bringing up the rear, and rhino-charge straight through it. We had no idea, of course, what lay on the other side of the fence.

CHAPTER FORTY-TWO

Considering that it would be far too dangerous to simply wander into the centre of Bo, we decided that a better option would be to make our way to Blossom's village. Once there we would be safe and able to dispatch someone to get help.

A military strategist, or indeed anyone who might know the first thing about planning operations, would probably criticise our proposal for being too simplistic, naive and almost certainly be doomed to failure. But we were determined and reminded ourselves, time and again that 'who dares wins', and, anyway, we didn't fancy another night in that hellhole.

Fred was already starting to get unusually grumpy – probably due to the appalling diet of nothing but rice, with indescribable chewy-stuff thrown in. He was almost twice my size so I surmised that that aspect of prison life hit him much harder than it did me.

Regardless of the risks, we were resolute. We were going to make a break for it, so we decided to be ready to go soon after midnight that night.

We lay on our bashas, nervous with anticipation, and waited for the next few hours to pass.

With the prison compound creating a break in the jungle canopy, a high level of moonlight, and plenty of cracks in the walls of our cell we were, just about, able to make out each other's faces.

I listened intently to the sentry as he slowly trudged around the small building, made his way back to the door and, with a slight cough, plonked himself back in his chair.

The time had come. All I needed to do then, was to create some sort of gentle distraction. The vice-chairman of the escape committee stood, circumspect by the weakened wall, eyes glued on my, barely visible, hand, waiting for my 'thumbs-up', as a sign for him to burst through the wall.

I emitted a sort of squeak, sounding something like a puppy in distress, or perhaps, a rusty gate in need of a squirt of oil, and scratched at the ground by the door.

I clearly heard the guard getting to his feet. Just as I was about to give the 'thumbs-up', he spoke.

I held back. A few seconds later, to my horror, I heard a second voice – and it was just as close as the first one.

I waved my hand frantically, ensuring that, at no time, did my thumb ever pass through the horizontal, and jumped to my feet.

"Stop. Stop. There are two of them," I whispered.

"Bollocks," came the reply.

There then ensued a two-way conversation from behind the door, interspersed with rounds of laughter.

It sounded almost as if the two of them were settled for the night, and enjoying each other's company, whilst tucking into a healthy dose of the local ganja.

We had no alternative, other than to abort our mission.

The next day we were down, but by no means out. We would try again that coming night.

Or so we thought.

As we lay on our bashas, swatting away the various types of flying bugs intent on settling onto any area of our exposed skin, and enduring the stifling heat of the day, the cell door opened.

Two guards, rifles at the ready, as usual, came in.

"Come. Come," one of them said.

We were lead towards the ramshackle shed which acted as the prison headquarters, the offices and the guards living accommodation.

The tiny office was empty apart from a desk and one chair, which was occupied by a man who was, clearly, a figure of authority. He was much better fed than anyone else in the camp and wore a uniform which looked as though it had recently been washed and ironed. On each shoulder, there were emblazoned two pips, donating the rank of a police inspector.

The inspector didn't look up, as the guards told us to stand in front of the desk. He spent time carefully reading from a notepad, which I assumed contained details of our 'crime' and 'criminal record' – or some such nonsense.

Eventually, he deigned to look up at us.

"Mister Marafano," he said with a smile. "You are free to leave. I hope your stay has not been too uncomfortable. Please give my regards to Chief Norman."

He turned his eyes towards me. "Mister Riley." This time said without a smile.

160

"You are free to proceed to Freetown only. Once there you will be required to appear in court to face charges relating to the illegal possession of diamonds."

He handed our rucksacks to us which, rather amazingly, still contained all our money, and said to us, "There is someone at the gate waiting to meet you. Goodbye."

That someone was Juba, the pilot. He shook our hands, in the, by now familiar, convoluted African manner, and then drove us towards Kenema, where the helicopter was waiting to fly us back to the capital.

On board was a cool-box containing enough food and drink for Fred and I and the four-man crew. The two of us tucked-in, and emptied the box almost before we got into the air.

As soon as we landed in Freetown I made straight for my hotel room. Without wasting a second I grabbed my passport and what few possessions I had and made my way to the airport.

My sole intention was to get out of the country before the police had time to get themselves organised and stop me from leaving.

The first flight displayed on the 'Departures' board was a Kenyan Airways flight to Nairobi, which was in completely the opposite direction to where I wanted to go. Having managed to elbow my way through the crowd and purchase a ticket, I sat nervously, in the chaotic departure lounge and waited for the flight to be called.

It wasn't until the following morning as I sat in the Business section of a British Airways Jumbo-Jet, on route from Nairobi to London, that I felt able to relax.

Some weeks later, back at home, on the edge of the West Pennine Moor, I received two letters from The Republic of Sierra Leone.

The first was from the Department of Justice in Freetown, instructing me to appear in court to face charges of 'Smuggling and Tax Evasion', crimes which carried a maximum sentence of twenty years' imprisonment.

The second, was from an associate of 'faithful George' (the same George who had betrayed us and ran off with our stash of diamonds), asking me to transfer the sum of two thousand dollars into his Western Union account. He explained that he had another friend who was a high-court judge, and upon receipt of the money he would be happy to represent me. He would, he said, be able to deal with the charges raised against me on my behalf, thereby saving my good reputation and the expenses of having to travel back to Africa.

Needless to say – I ignored both letters.

To this day, I have never returned to Sierra Leone, and what is more, I can honestly say that I hope I never will.

CHAPTER FORTY-THREE
BLOSSOM

After the RUF attack on the village outside Bo, Blossom's health, both physical and mental, deteriorated rapidly. Shortly after being released from prison, and working under the protective umbrella of Executive Outcomes, Fred visited the village and was shocked by the young woman's condition.

He was concerned that Blossom was close to death, and without any undue ceremony, picked up the emaciated girl, placed her in the Land Rover, and drove her to the hospital in Freetown.

With Blossom in his arms and his rifle slung across his powerful shoulders, Fred trudged into the hospital reception. He forced his way through the inevitable crowd and demanded that his charge was attended to immediately, and at whatever cost.

For more than a month Fred paid for Blossom to receive the best care available and arranged for food and water to be delivered to her regularly.

The monstrous attack Blossom had endured, and the savage murder of her baby daughter was not the first time she had been tortured at the hands of repulsive and barbaric human beings.

The Juju-man, sometimes known as the 'Barber-man', was always busy. He had a large area of responsibility, covering many villages, most of whose inhabitants were only too willing to pay for his services. The visits of the, very important, and powerful, Barber-man were always anticipated with great excitement.

Girls in the village as young as three-years-old were told that, when it was their turn to be treated by the Barber-man, it would be a joyous occasion and a time for much celebration.

The Witch Doctor was the only health-care worker available to the indigenous population and they were in awe of his ability to perform his wondrous acts which often bordered upon magic.

With long, matted dreadlocks, lion's canine teeth pierced through his earlobes, and a leopard skin draped across his shoulders, he portrayed a formidable and imposing figure. With just a shake of his Juju-stick or a rattle of his bone-filled coconut shell, he had been known to cure fevers or even AIDS. The fingernails on his right hand were carefully manicured, long and razor-sharp. His strong, white teeth had been filed to make them capable of effortlessly slicing through flesh.

At just seven years old Blossom had had to wait a long time for her big day to come, but with so many other young girls for the Barber-man to attend to she understood, and accepted the delay. She was happy and excited, as were her mother, grandmother and two favourite aunts as they lead her towards the 'operating table', a tree trunk by her front door.

The tiny, naked girl was held down by the four chattering women, as the Barber-man approached, performing a dance-like shuffle and unintelligible chant as he did so. Blossom began to feel embarrassed and afraid. She turned to her Mama who, by then enthralled by the atmosphere of the ceremony, simply pressed down more firmly on her daughter's thigh, causing her to cry with pain.

Little Blossom screamed and writhed as the well-practiced mutilator forced the fingers of his left hand inside her and pulled her apart.

As the four-woman team of restrainers worked together to hold their sacrificial lamb to the tree-trunk, a fifth one joined them, gagging the young girl to stifle her screams.

The Barber-man then went about his business, in the style for which he was famous, and widely respected. He located the victim's tiny clitoris and, nipping it deftly with his thumb and forefinger, stretched it towards him. With the razor-sharp fingernails of his right hand, he cut away the bloody clitoral-hood, much to the satisfaction of the audience.

Forcing the legs further apart he then bit off both the left and right labia and, with his mouth dripping with blood, spat them out onto his hand. He then proudly displayed the amputated flesh to the onlookers, who acknowledged his workmanship with smiles and nods of approval.

After stitching up the wound with thorns from an acacia tree, he ordered that Blossom should be carried away and the next patient should be prepared for treatment.

Blossoms collarbone was fractured during her desperate struggle, and she was left to consider the advice that a little discomfort was worth enduring if she were ever to become a woman.

Fred decided that a bunch of flowers, and a dish of her favourite cassava leaves and stuffed-orca, would be just the thing to cheer Blossom up. When he arrived at the ward she normally slept in, he found her bed to be empty. She had died during the night.

Right up to his death, many years later, Fred was convinced that Blossom had died from a broken heart, due to the hideous murder of her baby daughter Yaema.

CHAPTER FORTY-FOUR
SARDINIA AND PARIS

The main part of my job with SIS was infiltration and exfiltration of agents. Normally I put together contingency plans to provide escape routes for them out of countries around the globe, in the event of them becoming compromised, and their lives, or the lives of their close families, coming under threat.

I also worked closely with the 'Increment', a very small and most secretive element of Special Forces often referred to as 'The Wing', or RWW, Revolutionary Warfare Wing. There were many times over the previous few years when individuals or, more likely, four-man teams from the Increment needed to be inserted into a foreign country without passing through any official channels.

One such operation in the summer of 1997 springs to mind.

It was a fairly straightforward task. Fly into PATA, Pontrilas Army Training Area, just south of Hereford, with the civilian registered Agusta 109 helicopter, and make myself available to the Increment for the following few days.

I arranged to meet up with the 'Wing' sergeant major at nine o'clock the following morning, Tuesday the 19th of August, for a briefing.

Although there were fuel and accommodation available at PATA, I decided to fly down that evening and spend the night at a very pleasant hotel just outside Ross-On-Wye, where I could land on the front lawn and park up for the night. I arrived there in good time for dinner, a few drinks and a comfortable bed at the expense of Her Majesty.

As I lifted off the next morning I got a less than friendly wave from a naked man as I climbed slowly past his open bedroom window, before setting the course for the five-minute flight to Pontrilas.

The task was to get four members of RWW onto the island of Sardinia as discreetly as possible.

I decided that the best option was to take off, at about five that evening, and land at Compton Abbas Airfield in rural Dorset. From there the team and I would transfer to a small twin-engine aeroplane, with my old mate Richard as captain and myself as co-pilot, for the remainder of the route into a small airfield north of Cagliari, planning to arrive there just after last light.

The team turned up dressed, pretty much, in the standard rig for SAS soldiers at that time. Jeans, T-shirts, bomber jacket and each carrying a medium sized rucksack.

On any of these sorties I refrained from asking my passengers what was in their baggage – I didn't care. They were quite likely to be hauling surveillance equipment aids, radios or other technical devices and possibly weapons and explosives. As pilots, we paid no heed to the regulations imposed by the Civil Aviation Authorities regarding the carriage of Dangerous Air Cargo. Or any other regulations for that matter. We considered it was our job to simply get our passengers into a foreign country, with ultimate discretion in any way we could. And that is exactly what we usually managed to do. Most times we would file no flight plan and would fly at ultra-low level to avoid detection by radar. Flying over water in total darkness and displaying no lights we would never climb more than one hundred feet above the surface. Over land we would try to route down valleys in order to use the surrounding hills to provide protection from foreign Air Defence Systems.

After landing at the small, unlit, airfield on the outskirts of Cagliari, I quickly opened the door and, with the engines still running, the guys jumped out and disappeared into the night. The doors were immediately closed, take-off power applied, and we were on our way back to the UK after a visit of less than a minute.

Why a four man SAS team would want to sneak onto the island of Sardinia was no concern of ours. Richard and I parked up at Compton Abbas and made our way to the Fontmell pub in the village just down the road, for the usual drinks and a bed for the night.

Ten days later I was back in the same hotel near Ross-On-Wye tasked with a similar trip to the one to Sardinia. The following morning, I lifted off but was a little disappointed not to have the angry, naked man waving me off on my way to my next MI6 mission.

This time the task was for a different four-man team to be dropped off in a field just outside the French capital, Paris. I didn't consider it was necessary to use Richard's fixed wing aircraft for this trip. I would be able to get a quick squirt of fuel at Shoreham just before coasting out and, pop over to Paris and back, with just myself flying the helicopter.

An hour, or so, before darkness my four passengers arrived, looking remarkably like last week's bunch. Again, no questions were asked. Simply pile on board and wait to be dropped off in the field using no lights and Anvis Night Vision Goggles. (I was one of only a handful of pilots in the UK qualified to fly as single-crew using Night Vision Goggles). After a quick exit, the team again disappeared into the night and I made my way back to the airfield in Dorset where I was met by Richard and Clive, the airfield owner, who rushed me down to the pub before last orders.

The next day I was back at home, now divorced and living on my own. Just like millions of other people around the world, I was stunned when I turned on the radio and learned that Princess Diana and her partner Dodi Fayed, had been killed in a tragic car accident in Paris shortly after spending a few days on a yacht moored off the island of Sardinia.

CHAPTER FORTY-FIVE
EXFILTRATION OF NIMBUS

A text message, *'Morning hun all well with u after last night?? Love Sandra xx'*

The message is not from Sandra, it's from someone in the office in London. MI6 Headquarters by Vauxhall Bridge. It has come through on a cheap, pay-as-you-go mobile, which I keep with me at all times when I am on standby. This phone has no other purpose than to accept this kind of message from the office.

Sandra probably doesn't even exist, she or he, is more likely to be some *'shiny arse'* bloke. A *'shiny arse'* is someone who spends their working life sitting behind a desk, shining up the arse of their trousers. The sender of the message probably doesn't even know my real name or anything about me. Agents like myself are never allowed in MI6 Headquarters. We are normally referred to, within the hallowed corridors of Vauxhall, by a four-digit number or, occasionally, an allocated code name.

The text is simply a prearranged instruction for me to get in touch with the office via our secure communication system. I hazard a guess at what they want this time, probably just another bollocking for staying at the five-star Sheraton Hotel instead of the Holiday Inn during my last deployment, or flying first class, despite being told that all government agencies are having to tighten their belts. It has been repeatedly made clear to me that it is now SIS policy that all agents will, whenever possible, travel business or, better still, economy class. I must admit I do have the propensity to wind the 'shiny arses' up – a hangover from my military days I suppose. I always try to keep a straight face when I am being given the lecture about the benefits of flying economy class. How important it is for everyone to try to help the service make the best use of its meagre budget and not only that, I will be doing my bit for the whole of the UK economy. I smile and nod, mustering my most sincere expression. There is no way that I will be flying economy class. The lecturer knows that. I, of course, know that, and I know that he knows. I'm also pretty damn sure that he knows that I know that he knows.

I dig out one of the laptops issued to me. On the face of it, it is a bog-standard laptop accessible by a simple password, and once opened displays the usual apps and work found on most normal PCs or laptops. But this laptop is different, it contains a GCHQ cypher, which I am assured is almost impossible to crack and is absolutely impenetrable, unless you have access to the current CAKE. The Cypher Access Key Entry procedure is far more than just an alphanumerical password. It consists of an elaborate sequence of applications which I had to spend hours committing to memory. The CAKE, or any part of it, must not be written down under any circumstances. Access to the cypher by any unauthorised person could, not only, do serious damage to the infrastructure of SIS, endangering the lives of its agents and serving officers, but could seriously compromise the UK government itself.

I open the encrypted message. Short and sweet, *'Flat tomorrow 1400 briefing for deployment Tue.'* Well, that's good then, almost certainly not another bollocking unless that comes before the pre-deployment briefing, which has been known.

'The Flat', is what is often referred to in SIS circles as an OCP, an Operation Command Post. These rather quaint, jingoistic military terms are still prevalent throughout MI6, but *'The Flat'*, is just that – it's a flat. Her Majesty's Secret Intelligence Service rents a few flats, to be used as OCPs, within walking distance of Vauxhall Bridge, normally within the Pimlico area of London.

Our small group of agents designated the acronym UKD, United Kingdom Deniable, are all given keys and we all use *the flat* for briefings, stashing surplus equipment or clothing, or perhaps just somewhere to spend the night before, or after, deploying via London. We rarely keep the same flat for more than a year and it would cease to be used immediately if any one of us considered it to be compromised in any way.

Before leaving my home in Moreton-on-Lugg, a small village outside Hereford, I need to become a different person. I open the safe which is secreted in the back of my antique desk which was given to me by Sir David Stirling, founder of the Special Air Service who I worked for, for a short time after leaving the Army. In the safe there are four trays, each containing the paraphernalia needed to give credibility to any one of the four aliases I may wish to adopt; passport, driving licence, flying licences, mobile phone, credit and debit cards, club membership cards, business cards, wallet, watch, rings and anything else that I have allocated to belonging to that imaginary individual. I have four aliases allocated to me. They are, Robert Meacher, known as Bob, Robert Peter Grayling, also known as Bob and the final Bob, Robert Davidson. I also have at my disposal Peter John Elmond, who I call Pete. Surnames are allocated by the office. Christian names we normally tend to keep the same but, of course, there is always the exception to the rule.

I currently have two operational aliases, Grayling and Meacher. One training alias, Davidson and one work-in-progress alias, Elmond, which is an alias that can only be used operationally once much more background work has been completed.

An operational alias takes a considerable amount of time and effort to build up. The idea that a Mi6 agent would be deployed outside the United Kingdom, without having a robust and well-tested alias is bordering on ludicrous.

Bob Grayling has a genuine and well-thumbed UK passport, a driving licence with three penalty points for speeding and a bank account where the credit and debit cards are regularly used. He has an ACA, an Accommodation Cover Address, where he lives regularly with a family that has been carefully vetted and briefed by SIS. Bob is on the electoral role at his ACA. He visits the local pubs and restaurants keeping receipts and cards to be carried in the bottom of his bag or scrunched up in the corner of his pocket for whenever he is deployed abroad. He joins the library, the running and squash clubs, and he gets to know as much about the local area as possible. Anyone who gets to know Bob in and around where he lives is told, that he works overseas and rents a room from the vetted family when in the UK.

Mr Grayling also has a BCF, a Business Cover Facility. Once a suitable candidate, normally the head of a reasonably sized UK company, has been identified, the head and, possibly the managing director's PA, will be vetted and approached to provide the services of a Business Cover Facility. The head of Bob's BCF has a private jet, a helicopter and runs a business with interests across the globe which suits him perfectly. He can be notionally employed as, say, chief pilot or a sales manager with all the business cards, brochures, letters and bits and pieces which help to build up a credible employment background.

On his mobile phone are numbers, text messages and emails relating to his job as a chief pilot at Grampian Aviation Limited. Bob's girlfriend is Donna, who he communicates with regularly and sometimes in ways that he would prefer to remain private, in just the same way that most couples might do.

All this background work is put into place to avoid a foreign official becoming suspicious if he should come across an individual, Billy-no-mates with a brand-new passport, no messages or texts on his phone or laptop and he doesn't even know the name of the pub just around the corner from where he is supposed to live.

The training alias has just a shallow cover and is used within the United Kingdom only.

Since I am only planning to go to London, I swap my real cards and things for the stuff in the training alias tray and –

"Today Mathew, I am going to be Bob Davidson."

CHAPTER FORTY-SIX

Bob arrives at Paddington Station just a little after 11.30 am, leaving him plenty of time to walk the forty minutes or so to the flat in Lupus Street, Pimlico. He's the first one there so gets on with the most important job of the day – check that there is enough brew kit available. Hard to tell how many people will turn up for the briefing, could be as many as twenty or as few as two. The number attending depends entirely upon the nature of the job. As it happens there is a total of six today, so no worries about the catering arrangements, the half empty container of milk should see us through nicely.

Apart from Bob, there is his oldest mate within the group, Richard. Richard, like Bob, is a professional pilot, both are highly experienced and hold Airline Transport Pilots Licences for both fixed and rotary wing aircraft. With a total of more than twenty thousand flying hours between them, they make a formidable aviation team. Generally, Bob tends to look after any helicopter flying requirements and leaves the fixed wing to Richard. There is Mike, the Royal Air Force Liaison Officer, a serving wing commander on a three-year secondment to SIS. Neil the Security Officer who tends to get involved with most operations will also be at the meeting. His remit is to maintain an overview of the wider aspects of security and will get his two pennies worth in only if he feels security is being exposed to too high a risk; and there is Robin, a UKD 'shiny arse' whose job it is to keep Bob and Richard under control, with very limited success. Lastly, there is David the case officer. He is a regular full-time intelligence officer who will be heading the briefing and will be responsible for the overall operation if it is eventually sanctioned and goes ahead.

Any operations to be carried out abroad must receive ministerial approval before they can get underway and will only be sanctioned once the detailed plans and risk assessments have been considered by the minister.

David starts the briefing with the usual first-things-first. Curtains closed, television on with volume up, but not too loud, all mobile phones on the table with batteries removed.

Although everyone is known to each other, David, firstly, introduces himself then points to each one in turn for them to introduce themselves. Christian names and role within the organisation are all that is needed.

David opens the briefing, "Gents... Sorry, Robin," he corrects himself, "*Lady* and Gents, thank you for coming." He scribbles on the whiteboard next to him, 'OPERATION CASTAWAY', and underlines it twice. "For the past two years or so we have been running an agent in Libya, code name Nimbus who, from now on, will be referred to as Charlie One." He pauses and sticks a mugshot of Nimbus on to the board.

"Charlie One is a nuclear scientist who is trusted by and works closely with, Colonel Muammar Qadafi himself. He is married to Amelia, Charlie Two, and has two sons – Josef, Charlie Three, who has just turned eighteen and about to start university, and finally, Ismal, Charlie Four, who is sixteen." David again remains silent as he sticks another three photographs of the subjects onto the whiteboard.

"The Colonel is going to be seriously pissed off if – or more likely when – he finds out that Charlie One has been keeping the UK government in the loop regarding Libya's nuclear weapons development programme," he says reaching for his notes.

"We, as a service, consider that that time is now fairly close and we have a responsibility and a duty of care to protect Charlie One and his family." David clears his throat and glances around the room as if addressing each one of us in turn.

"Libyan nuclear scientists, and the like, are rarely allowed out of the country without being very closely chaperoned by Moussa Koussa's heavies. Koussa, by the way, is head of Mukhabarat el-Jamahiriya, the Libyan Intelligence Service'. A fifth photograph, this time of Koussa is added to the gallery.

"The measure of the close relationship between Qadafi and Charlie One is clear from the fact that, not only has government approval been granted for him to travel to Syria next week for a meeting with President Assad, but he is also being allowed to take his family with him and arrangements have been made for Charlie Three to visit Damascus University, with a view to him starting there later this year." He pauses as if to accentuate the gravity of what we are likely to become involved in.

"This is a once in a lifetime opportunity for us to get the whole family to safety, and I would ask you all to get your heads together for the next hour or so and come up with an outline exfiltration plan. Please bear in mind that the family arrives in Damascus in just three days' time, and are scheduled to stay for a maximum of seven nights. We have already considered the land and sea options but because of the short window of opportunity, the consensus is that it must be an extraction by air or nothing." David closes his notepad indicating that the briefing has finished. "Whilst you get started I will get the kettle on. Just shout up if anything other than NATO-standard coffee is required."

CHAPTER FORTY-SEVEN

In less than an hour, we have an outline plan. If station staff in Damascus can recce at least two isolated helicopter landing sites, suitable for night operations, within about ten miles from the city centre, and they can also get the family to meet up with the *'Heli'*, then the extraction can go ahead.

Richard will pre-position the King Air 350, and Bob the Agusta 109 helicopter to the Royal Air Force Station Akrotiri in Cyprus on the same day that the family are due to arrive in Syria. On a chosen night, when the weather is deemed to be acceptable for ultra-low level flying over the mountainous terrain of the Lebanon, using no lights and night vision goggles, Bob will fly in from Cyprus and meet up with the vehicle transporting the family to the HLS from their hotel. He will then do a quick arse-about-face back to Akrotiri, where the family will be flown back to the UK by Richard in the King Air. What could be simpler?

After listening to our outline plan David ponders for a few seconds then says thoughtfully.

"Ok. I can sort out the Damascus side of things so let's get cracking. Bob, yours sounds like the trickiest bit, so you take the lead for the planning please. Give me more detail about your side of the operation and I will put the plans in place for the team on the ground to get the family to the landing site at the right time."

Bearing in mind the 'seven Ps principle' – *prior planning and preparation prevents piss poor performance!* – drummed into us by the military, we get our heads together.

Just before seven o'clock, we have a more detailed plan which we feel has a reasonable chance of success.

The fixed wing side of things is straightforward. Richard will fly, with one of the members of the group of UKD agents as co-pilot, into RAF Akrotiri after taking a refuelling stop in Italy, and simply sit and wait until required for the transit back to the UK. Upon arrival at Lydd Airport in

Kent, he will be met by an RAF helicopter flown by our old mate Lex from the S and D Flight who are normally based in RAF Odiham. The family will then be flown into the garden of a safe house for processing. As soon as the operation is given the go ahead, Bob will set off in the Agusta 109 with another member of the group, Simon, as a co-pilot planning three refuel stops en route. Simon will carry the appropriate cover of a Film Production Location Manager, working on a planned documentary about the troubles in the Middle East.

For the duration of the operation, Bob will become Captain Robert Grayling, chief pilot of Grampion Aviation Limited, who have been commissioned by the film company for aerial photography around Lebanon, Israel and the Golan Heights.

The team on the ground must select a minimum of two landing sites, no further east than the centre of Damascus since the limited range of the helicopter is crucial and any further east would leave it with insufficient fuel for the return leg.

The distance from Akrotiri to Damascus is a little over two hundred nautical miles. With a mountain range rising to almost ten thousand feet to navigate across, and with a total distance of over four hundred and fifty nautical miles to fly, the 109 will be left with a reserve of only ten minutes flying time and very little room for error. After take-off, all lights will be extinguished, and the route will be flown at less than one hundred feet above the surface using the Anvis Night Vision Goggles.

Shortly after take-off, the QRF, 'Quick Reaction Force', a heavily armed team of six professional soldiers will get airborne and fly close to the limits of Cypriot-controlled airspace, ready to fly into the landing site if given a coded message, 'Zulu, Zulu'. The message, which will be passed from Bob, will indicate the team are in imminent danger and request assistance to fight their way out to safety.

The Search and Rescue helicopter will also be put on immediate standby ready to launch should the 109's ten-minute reserve diminish to zero, and a night-ditching into the Mediterranean become necessary.

The preferred landing site will be designated 'Alpha'. Should the site be compromised then any member of the team will transmit, 'Zulu Zulu' over the secure communications system and the pick-up will be transferred to the backup site 'Delta'.

Mike, the RAF liaison officer, will make all the arrangements with the station commander in Akrotiri for any essential support including preparing the SAR and QRF teams, and the supply of personal weapons for Bob and Simon. Both of whom request Heckler and Koch HK-53s and Walther PPK pistols with calf holsters and two full magazines for each weapon.

David nods intermittently as he scribbles away on his notepad then, as if for theatrical effect, emphasises coming to a close, with a large full stop.

"Right, that's all done then," he says. 'I will get that all written up and aim to have it on the Minister's desk by nine o'clock tomorrow morning. Oh, yes, one last thing, Bob, what would you put as the EMSR for this operation?"

"Err, pardon, the EMS what?" I mumble. "Oh, yes, of course, that! Umm."

Just as my jaw begins to drop and my eyes glaze over, Richard comes to my rescue.

"We have given this considerable thought, and in our opinion," he says with an air of confidence.

'Why the fuck has his voice become so affected?' I think to myself.

"We would put the Estimated Mission Success Ratio as somewhere between fairly slim, and no fucking chance whatsoever! My part of the job is simple, but if Bob manages to pull his part off then he doesn't deserve a medal. He deserves a fucking knighthood!"

"Oh... ah... well', says David. "I will put that down as fifty-fifty then."

As usual, Richard and I are the only ones to laugh.

It's almost midnight before I get back home, open the safe and lay Bob Davidson to rest on his tray.

Just before ten o'clock the following morning I get another text from Sandra. I open the secure communications on my laptop.

'Ministerial approval granted.'

'Operation Castaway is on!'

CHAPTER FORTY-EIGHT

Before deploying on any operation, I have, what I call, the *'Dry Cleaning'*, ritual to perform. Anything that is going with me such as; bags, clothes, documentation, brochures, letters, books. In fact, anything at all is put to one side. I search through every corner of the bags, every pocket of every jacket or pair of trousers, leaf through every piece of paper and every page of every book.

That done, I feel confident that there is nothing hidden away that might expose my true identity to any inquisitive foreign official. I then plant the bits and pieces that will hopefully, convince anyone rummaging through my kit that I am who I say I am. On this occasion, I will be Captain Robert Grayling, chief pilot of Grampian Aviation Limited.

Upon arrival at the hangar, Simon and I check out each other's stories. How do we know each other? When did we first meet? Do we have any similar passport entries and dates? With no apparent evidence to contradict us, we decide that this is the first time we have ever met and therefore we know very little about each other.

We meet up with David, Mike, and of course, Richard in a small room within the underground operations centre of the RAF station. David confirms that the family have landed safely and are now on their way to the Four Seasons Hotel on Shukri al-Quwatli Street in downtown Damascus, and it is believed, but by no means certain, that Charlie One has a couple of meetings tomorrow but, as yet, no evening engagements.

Mike informs us that we have been allocated rooms in the officers' mess and that he will deliver the weapons and ammunition to our rooms later. He makes it clear that any facilities of the operations centre, including the Met Office, are completely at our disposal.

I look at the forecast weather chart on the desk in front of me for a few seconds.

"Looks to me like the high-pressure system dominating the whole area is likely to stick around for, at least the next day or two," I say after studying the chart.

"Tomorrow may be the only evening when the whole family are not tied up with social engagements, so... if the guys on the ground can get their act together at such short notice, then I reckon we should aim to lift off straight after last light tomorrow."

David gives a little nod.

"I agree. We simply cannot risk having them out with the diplomats till all hours of the night, or the weather taking a turn for the worse, and before we know it they will be on the plane back to Tripoli. So, let's strike while the iron is hot."

We all agree that an early night would be a very sensible course of action but, of course, it doesn't happen. Instead, we finish up in the bar of the officers' mess staying until closing time and staggering off to bed well after midnight.

CHAPTER FORTY-NINE

It's a glorious sunset on the very southern tip of the island of Cyprus as we wait for total darkness and a call from David to confirm when we are good to go.

We have ripped any unnecessary luxuries out of the back of the helicopter including; bar, drinks cabinet, soft seats and even carpets, to reduce the weight as much as possible. We are just under the maximum allowable take-off weight here on the runway. By the time we get to the pick-up point we will have burnt about two hundred and fifty kilogrammes of Jet A1 fuel, otherwise known as Avtur. With four passengers jumping on board and the landing site being at about four thousand feet above sea level, we are going to be some way over weight for take-off. But I know this aircraft well and I am confident that, with gentle handling, we will be able to get airborne safely.

The outside of the helicopter has also been prepared. The judicious application of a little matt black paint here and there has made the last three letters of the aircraft registration indecipherable. The first letter is perfectly clear, that is an 'N' meaning that it is registered in the USA. In the unlikely event of anyone catching a glimpse of us then it is most likely to be reported that we are American. And if the pesky Americans get to take the flack for illegally flying into a sovereign state's airspace, then that suits us just fine!

We have no need for maps or charts. We have studied this route meticulously and Simon has jotted a few notes on his kneepad to back up the GPS, should it fail. He has noted just the heading we need to hold till coasting into the south of Beirut, and the time we should pass to the north of Lake Bagram in the hills just west of Damascus. He will them adjust the heading and time if required to run in to the landing site. Flying at less than one hundred feet using NVG requires intense concentration and a constant lookout. There is no time for looking inside the cockpit reading maps or charts. The night vision goggles we are using are the best available and allow us excellent images of the surface, albeit in only differing shades of green. Lights stand out exceptionally well and can be seen from much further away than with the mark one eyeball.

The coded message comes in from David.

"The team are on their way to the pick-up point with Charlie One and family and we are good to go."

I raise the collective lever to apply sufficient power to lift off to a height of four feet above the ground. I check the engine temperatures, oil pressures, and the amount of torque I am having to apply to maintain the hover. This indicates the margin of power I have in reserve – not much! It's a fairly cool night for this part of the world, just under plus ten degrees Celsius. This helps a lot since the lower the ambient temperature the better the aircraft performance.

I turn on to our initial south-easterly heading which I will endeavour to maintain as accurately as possible until we cross the coast to the south of Beirut and five miles north of Saida. I set the cruise power at ninety percent which will give us about one hundred and fifty knots and, as Simon raises the landing gear, I level off at one hundred feet. The trick now is to maintain this flying configuration as precisely as I can and with any luck, we should pass just to the north of Lake Bagram as planned.

Once clear of the Cyprus coast I call for Simon to switch off all the lights, the Civilian Air Traffic Control radio, and the transponder. If left on the transponder will show Air Traffic Control our position, altitude and our registration. With it off they will, hopefully, see nothing. We have no intentions of speaking to any Air Traffic Control authorities in Lebanon or Syria, so the radio is left off and any communications from now on will only be over the secure network.

I set the radar altimeter to fifty feet, which will then flash a warning light if we descend to below that height, indicating that we are getting dangerously low.

I am working hard to concentrate on holding everything as steady as possible and maintain a good lookout. We are low enough to hit even a small fishing boat and at this speed, I would have only a second or two to take avoiding action. The sea is flat calm and with nothing but a dull green panorama ahead of me I struggle to keep changing the focus of my eyes to avoid a phenomenon known as empty-field myopia. This is a condition where, if the eyes have nothing to focus on, will gradually focus just a few metres ahead. This short focal range will not only mean, that I will not see that tiny fishing boat until the very last second, but it can also lead to spatial disorientation, a very dangerous condition for even the most experienced of pilots to cope with.

I know that at this ultra-low level, due to the curvature of the earth, the horizon is about twelve miles away, but with the mountains, the built-up areas and good visibility we should start to pick out the lights of Beirut and its environs at a range of fifty miles or so.

Simon is the first to spot what appears to be a radio mast on a hill in our eleven o'clock position. Over the next few minutes, the lights of the city and the mountains in the background start to become clear.

The silence is broken by, "Golf Golf, Quebec airborne standing by."

This indicates to us that the QRF helicopter is now lurking at the edge of Lebanese airspace and ready to get us out of the shit if needed.

"Roger that," Simon replies.

We cross the coastline about five miles to the north of the town of Saida, pretty much on track, and start to climb to cross the mountain range twenty miles, or so, ahead.

"Once we get to the top of this hill, give the guys on the ground a call please mate," I ask Simon.

"Will do, skipper," he replies. "We seem to be more or less on track at the moment. Not bad for a pongo. The way you held that course over the ogin was getting close to Royal Marines standards.' He teases me. Royal Marines invariably refer to the sea as 'the ogin and anyone in the Army as a pogo.'

I smile but continue to concentrate, finding it more difficult to maintain a constant height above ground as we climb steeply, our airspeed dropping to only one hundred knots.

As we pass over the hill – which is, in fact, an eight-thousand-foot ridge line – Simon presses the transmit button with his foot. "Alpha Alpha two zero." Meaning that we will be at landing site Alpha in twenty minutes. "Roger Roger Alpha two zero," comes the reply.

Great. That means that the ground party with the family will be there at the same time. Happy days, things are looking good. But not for long. Five minutes later, the shit hits the fan!

CHAPTER FIFTY

Just as I'm asking Simon if he can see flashing lights in the vicinity of the landing site, the radio burst into life.

"Zulu Zulu Alpha fucking crawling with Zulus!"

Not quite the standard of radio procedure we would hope for but it certainly gets the message across – the landing site we have called Alpha is full of unwanted guests, most likely police or Army.

"Roger that revert to Delta send ETA Over," I reply.

Simon gives me a new heading for landing site Delta, which is now only five minutes flying time away.

A female voice comes over the radio with the sound of a screaming engine in the background. "Delta, Delta two zero with any luck, but think we are being followed!"

"Roger. Pretty sure we can see you, and yes, it looks like there are flashing lights a mile or so behind you," Simon replies.

I slow down to sixty knots to use less power and therefore less fuel. Don't want to land too early, and the change of locations is already eating into our meagre reserve of ten minutes flying time.

As we identify the landing site at a range of about two miles we can now clearly see the rapidly approaching vehicle, a Toyota Land Cruiser, and a convoy of three vehicles with, what we assume are, blue flashing lights, but, of course, they just look a different shade of green to us.

I time the landing in order for us to be on the ground just a few seconds before the first vehicle arrives.

"Don't waste any time. Zulus are right up your arse!" I scream into the radio.

Simon is out of the aircraft in a flash, HK-53 in his right hand and his left holding the rear door open. The Land Cruiser screeches to a halt in a cloud of dust only feet away. The doors fly open and six people stumble out and dash towards Simon.

As everyone is piling into the back, the first of the Zulus arrive, with the next two rapidly approaching. Two figures, which I guess are police, brandish their pistols and start to take un-aimed shots towards us. Simon reacts immediately, two bursts from his Heckler and Koch send the police officers scurrying behind their vehicle.

Simon is back on board with the six passengers, two more than we expected, crammed into the back.

"Let's get the fuck out of here!" shouts Simon, as he sticks his weapon far enough out of the window to avoid red-hot spent cartridges rattling around the cockpit, the last thing we need right now, as he sends another couple of bursts of automatic fire towards the police vehicles.

Getting the fuck out of here is easier said than done. We are now way over our maximum take-off weight and a quick lift-off just isn't possible. The only way to get airborne is by using a technique known as a 'cushion creep' to *very gently* ease forward at no more than four feet from the ground and then dive over the edge of the plateau. We can now only hope to pick up sufficient airspeed to give us the lift we need before hitting the bottom of the valley. The technique works, the airspeed steadily increases. Simon gets the landing gear up and we slowly gain height. I am now able to pull sufficient power to, just about, get us over the ridge and towards the Mediterranean.

"Well, wasn't that fun. Just like being back in the mob," Simon says with a chuckle.

"Not over yet, I'm afraid mate," I reply. "With the extra two passengers we are having to burn more fuel and I reckon there is a reasonable chance we could be taking a quick dip before the night is over."

A long period of silence follows as I contemplate the options and, I guess, Simon is doing the same. With a fraction over two hundred kilogrammes of fuel remaining in the two main tanks, and the auxiliary tank completely empty, according to the gauges. We still have over one hundred and sixty miles to run, one hundred of them over water, and I calculate that leaves us about ten miles short. Fuel gauges are not entirely accurate and are usually set to under-read slightly, but I can't be certain.

I decide to go for it.

I call the QRF, "Quebec Quebec this is Golf. Charlie safely extracted. Returning to base Over."

"Roger that. Standing down. See you there," comes the reply.

For the next forty minutes, or so, we both sit in silence spending far more time looking at the fuel gauges than we do looking ahead.

With fifty miles to run, the Fuel Low warning lights flash on. According to the flight manual, this means we now have fifteen minutes flying time to empty tanks. By my calculation, it will take us twenty minutes to reach dry land.

I climb to five hundred feet above the sea and tell Simon to put the lights and transponder on. We are now in Cypriot Airspace and it is time for us to be seen.

I call up Search and Rescue who, I very much hope, are standing by.

"Sierra Sierra this is Golf Check." ... Silence.

After a few seconds, I try again, "Sierra Sierra this is Golf Check." Still nothing more than a sickening silence.

"Fuck! Fuck! Fuck!" we both say almost in harmony, causing us both to laugh nervously.

"Typical fucking 'crabs' probably pissing it up in the Mess with Richard," chunters Simon.

Then comes the message like manna from heaven, "Golf Golf this is Sierra. Sorry about the delay, was on the wrong radio."

"Roger that Sierra no problem. We have thirty-four miles to run, very low on fuel and a ditching possible in ten minutes or so. We have eight souls on board," I say.

"Roger. Airborne now. Will tuck in behind you. Good luck."

Our fifteen minutes flying time are up. We can see the land and the air-field four miles ahead. The Search and Rescue helicopter has taken up a position in our five o'clock. Tantalisingly close. All we can do now is wait for things to go very quiet.

CHAPTER FIFTY-ONE

Eighteen minutes and forty seconds after the Fuel Low warning lights came on, the number one engine stops. I am anticipating this and I know we are still able to fly with one engine out, but not for long. The number one engine has always run a little bit hotter and a little bit faster than the number two engine and therefore, by my reckoning, must surely use more fuel. I am confident that over the two hours and fifty minutes we have been flying, we must have at least two minutes' fuel left in tank number two.

And one minute is all I need.

Less than a mile now to dry land. Surely if we ditch now we will be able to step out and walk to the shore hardly getting our feet wet. The engine continues to run and we land on the very first metre of concrete available. We taxi along the runway and towards the dispersal area, where there are three vehicles and a small crowd of people, including David, Mike and, of course, Richard. Before getting into the waiting people carrier, Nimbus's family, and even the unwelcome illegal stowaways, who should by now be back in the British Embassy in Damascus, also insist on giving me not one, but two, sloppy, garlic-laden kisses, on each cheek and enthusiastic handshakes. I decide to draw the line when Simon and Richard start to approach me with puckered lips. Kisses from an ex-Royal Marine and an ex-Paratrooper, as nice as they might be, are not something that I am keen to experience!

"Bloody good job mate," says Richard as he slaps me on the back. "The debrief can wait till tomorrow. Let's get to the mess before the bar closes."

We dump our weapons in our rooms, and head for the bar, where Richard is already waiting. He hasn't ordered any drinks yet because that can't be done without him first having an audience.

"Take a seat chaps and allow me the honour of buying you all a beverage. Three of your finest ales good man."

"His voice has gone all weird again!"

"And for myself, a glass of fresh raspberry juice. Important that I keep

187

myself in tip-top condition for flying tomorrow," he says to the bewildered-looking barman.

'Sorry sir, but we don't have any fresh raspberry juice," says the barman.

"Oh dear, make it a large Grouse then, with a splash of water."

We've all heard it before but it makes us laugh nevertheless, probably a bit louder than necessary, but I for one can feel the tension slipping away.

CHAPTER FIFTY-TWO
OPERATION DRUGSTORE

Richard, my close friend and fellow agent in MI6, rang me and asked if I could meet up with him without delay. He was at his house in the West Country, and I was at my Accommodation Cover Address (ACA), almost three hundred miles away in Lancaster. We could both have travelled to the flat in London and met, but neither of us fancied the tedious train journey and overnight stay. I had the helicopter with me, so I agreed to fly down and meet him in his local village of Pimperne, a mile or so, outside Blandford Forum in Dorset.

"Great," said Richard. "There's a bit of grass by the Farquharson Arms in the village. Let me know when you get there and I'll treat you to dinner."

"Hang on for a second," I replied as I reached for my map of UK. "This bit of grass. Is it big enough to land on? Are there any tables and chairs on it? I can't just roll up unless I know the landing site is suitable."

"I've got squirrels in my loft, so I can't get down there just yet," he said. "Give Kevin, the landlord, a bell and he'll make sure it's clear for you."

"*Squirrels in my loft?*" – I had not the faintest idea what that had to do with anything, and I didn't ask. I just rang the landlord anyway.

Kevin was a Dorset man through and through. He had a very strong, slow, drawn-out accent. He had lived in Pimperne all his life, as had his parents, and probably their parents before them. He had never in his forty or so years travelled outside of the county.

"Why would I be wannin' to go to London?" he would say. "Can't get nothin' ther' that I can't be gettin' in Blanford."

The conversation I had with Kevin was not easy.

"Can I land on the grass by the side of the pub later this evening?"

"Well, I suppose yer' cud if yer' ad an elicopter or summert."

"Yes Kevin, I do have a helicopter. How big is the grassed area?"

"Oh well now… that whole thing is quite big, but it's not that big."

"Are there any tables or chairs on it?"

"Not now there ain't. I been cuttin' that bloody grass all mornin'. So, I ave."

"That's great. Does it have much of a slope on it?"

"Well, that's the odd thing. When I look from ere there's not much of a slope. But when I'm cuttin' it there be one 'ell of a slope."

I began to feel as though I was losing the will to live.

"Thanks, Kevin'. I said as I tried to imagine what the landing site might be like. 'I'll be there at about six o'clock. Please don't put any tables or chairs out."

"Right-oh. See u tonight my lovely," he replied cheerfully.

Grant and Trish, my ACA keepers noticed me chuckling to myself as I put my phone away.

"Sorry, but I won't be able to hang around for dinner tonight. I'm off to deepest, darkest Dorset," I said.

As part of my cover for my alias Bob Grayling, Grant and Trish provided me with an address at which I often stayed. Grant had once served in the Royal Marines as a commando engineer and then worked at the Heysham nuclear power station. His wife Trish was a primary school teacher. They provided the vital services of an ACA for nothing more than a desire to support their country and a few, rather expensive, meals that I would pay for each year.

They were quite used to me coming and going at short notice so they were totally relaxed about me having to leave before the barbeque, planned for later that evening, got started.

The 'bit of grass', really was just that. Only just big enough to land on, and the slope was at the very limit of the helicopter's capability. It took me a little while to gently blow the tables and chairs, which Kevin had assured me would not be there, into the hedgerow. That way they couldn't be picked up by the rotor downwash and possibly damage the aircraft – not the type of landing procedure that the Civil Aviation Authority would have been too happy about. Richard and Kevin were standing by the window, smiling, and gave me a gentle handclap as I closed-down the engines and headed for the bar.

We did the usual Secret Agent stuff. Found a quiet table, and sat with our backs to the wall, where we could observe the entrances and the rest of the customers, but we passed on the recommended 'agent meeting protocol' bullshit.

Richard went on to tell me what was so important. He had been put in charge of a recently approved operation, and he had asked for me to be allocated to it as his second-in-command. The name of the operation was 'Drugstore', and the aim of Drugstore was to identify, and neutralise the capabilities of, an unknown nuclear scientist. The nuclear scientist was known to have established a proliferation organisation which was determined to develop what he called 'The Islamic Bomb'. International intelligence sources indicated that he was well on his way to success.

The importance of this operation was such that we would not be subjected to the normally strict controls from our office in London, but would instead answer directly to 'C', the head of the Secret Intelligence Service. Most unusually, there would be no budgetary constraints, and any resources we may need would be made available to us.

The nuclear scientist was given the code name 'Verger'. Our job was to identify Verger and disrupt his proliferation organisation. We made a solemn promise, in that quaint little corner of Dorset, that no matter what the cost, and regardless of any legal or moral niceties, he was going to be stopped – once and for all.

CHAPTER FIFTY-THREE

A few days after our meeting in Pimperne we sat down in the flat in Pimlico, London, to read through any intelligence briefings we could lay our hands on, and consider where it might be best to start.

There were two known protagonists in the area of Islamic Nuclear Proliferation, both, highly regarded, Pakistani nuclear physicists. Bashiruddin Mahmood and Abdul Qudeer Khan were both known to actively support the development of a nuclear weapon, which would not be controlled by a nation state but held in the name of Allah. There was no doubt that either Mahmood or Khan were suitably qualified to mastermind such an undertaking.

The intelligence reports showed that A.Q. Khan was known as the 'Father of The Islamic Bomb', and Mahmood had recently met with Osama bin Laden who had left him in no doubt that the Taliban leader was desperate to get his hands on a nuclear weapon of any sort. It was also a very realistic possibility that the whole project was being backed by the governments of North Korea and Colonel Gaddafi's Libya. Best guesses were that a third, as yet unknown advocate, with a much lower profile than the others, had been recruited and cultivated, to drive the enterprise forward. That third man was Verger.

On the list of many individuals who were noted as being of special interest to the intelligence services, there was one who we thought we should investigate further.

Jamil Riaz was thirty-eight-years old and hailed from Haripur, just North of Islamabad. He had gained a first-class honours degree from the University of Manchester Institute of Science and Technology and had then taken up a position at the Pakistan Atomic Energy Commission. For the past three years, nothing had been noted, other than the fact that he had, quite recently, originated some emails from an office in Dubai belonging to Global Exports Limited. GEL was also on a watch-list of companies from across the world whose activities, were considered to be worthy of suspicion.

Richard set to work establishing a company based in a hangar on the South Side of Bournemouth Airport, purporting to buy and sell aircraft spares and components from the Far and the Middle East and the UK. In the meantime, I would fly out to Dubai to take a look at the offices of Global Exports Limited.

Since we were not restricted by the normal budgetary constraints, and as a well-heeled individual and director of an international company, I thought that it would be only right and proper, to fly first-class on the Emirates flight to Dubai out of London Heathrow.

In keeping with my image as an international businessman, I booked into the Four Points Sheraton in Bur Dubai, just a short walk from the registered offices of GEL in the Al Musalla Towers.

At the reception desk of the, rather smart, Al Musalla Towers I told the guard that I was interested in business premises to rent. There were several offices available throughout the tower block and, after waiting for a couple of minutes, a young woman who spoke perfect English, arrived to show me around. After looking at a couple of properties on the way up through the building, we arrived at the fourth floor which consisted of only two suites of offices. One suite was empty and available for rent. The other suite was occupied, and emblazoned across the double oak doors was a large sign with gold letters – 'Global Exports Limited'. Our luck was in!

We paid for a year's rent in advance, and we also took four rooms in the Sheraton on a rolling monthly arrangement. Most of our days were spent in our new offices watching the comings and goings of our next-door neighbours. Within a week, or so, we had good photographs of six men, all of them of Asian appearance, and all falling within the age bracket of thirty to forty years old. Dressing smartly each day with clean white shirts and ties, they all seemed to work regular hours from Sunday to Thursday, the normal working week for that part of the world. During the weekends of Friday and Saturday the offices were generally empty and locked. Access to the offices could only be gained by swiping a key card across the entry pad.

We numbered the men from one to six, thinking that numbers one and two best fitted the age of Jamil Riaz who we knew to be about thirty-eight. The old mugshots we had been given of Riaz were of little help since any of the six could quite easily have fitted the appearance.

There were only two parking spaces allocated to each office suite in the basement of Al Musalla Towers and, our numbers 'one' and 'two' parked in them regularly, indicating to us that they were likely to be the senior members of staff.

Our two prime suspects were targeted with what we called a 'grabber'. A 'grabber' was a technical device, normally secreted in something like a laptop carrier, and when held within about a metre of someone could 'grab' the data from their mobile phone, credit cards or electronic passkeys. Once the data from any phones or cards had been harvested it was then sent back to London. GCHQ would then be able to monitor, or even control, every message or conversation on the mobile, and our technical guys in Vauxhall would be able to reproduce as many passkeys as they wanted. By standing close to the targets, usually in the lifts coming up from the basement car-park, we were easily able to grab all the data we needed.

Once passkeys had been produced, two of our 'Techies' joined us in Dubai. With Richard and I providing an early-warning system they carried out what we called a 'technical attack' on GEL's premises.

For the following six months, the directors of Service Air, as Richard had called our company; GCHQ in Cheltenham; and our Techies back in London, were privy to every conversation, message or phone call made from the offices next to ours. We even had real-time video coverage which was being transmitted back to our home-base twenty-four hours a day.

After the six months of continuous surveillance, we were then certain that GEL was involved in the acquisition of materials necessary to produce a nuclear weapon. Hard evidence showed that Colonel Gaddafi of Libya was also directly involved. There was then no doubt at all that number 'two' was Jamil Raiz, there was no doubt either that Raiz was Verger, and he was going to be stopped.

CHAPTER FIFTY-FOUR

Verger's intent to produce a nuclear weapon which could, quite possibly, end up in the hands of one such as Osama bin Laden, made him one of the most significant terrorists of that era.

We read his emails confirming that he was booked onto a flight to Geneva, where he would stay in the Mandarin Oriental hotel for five nights, and then fly on to Jakarta. Verger's wife was Indonesian and lived in Surabaya with their two children.

Richard was beginning to feel very unwell so we decided to fly to London a couple of days prior to Verger's planned trip, in order for him to receive medical attention. Upon arrival, Richard went straight off to see a doctor and I met up with Roger, another of our UKD operators. Later that day we flew to Geneva and checked ourselves into the Mandarin Oriental for a week.

Standing by her trolley in the corridor the young housekeeper, smiling politely, must have had me down as some sort of dirty old man, as I sidled up to her with my laptop bag slung over my shoulder. I couldn't tell her of course, but all I wanted to do was get close to her. Close enough for my 'grabber' to get inside her apron pouch. After a few seconds, my crutch started to twitch. It was the switch in my trouser pocket which was vibrating and telling me that the data from the housekeeper's skeleton-key had been successfully collected.

As soon as we were sure that the arch bombmaker had left the hotel and was well on his way to his meeting we entered his hotel room armed with what we intended to bring about his demise with – a camera.

We took close-up pictures of all his personal belongings, especially anything he had left in the bathroom; antiperspirant spray, medication, toothbrush, toothpaste, mouthwash, razor, shaving gel, eye-drops and aftershave lotion. The pictures were then transmitted back to our headquarters in Vauxhall.

Two days later we met with an agent in Starbucks on the waterfront. The agent had brought a package for us via diplomatic bag from London. He handed us the large brown envelope which contained a wooden box, similar to one which might contain a high-quality handgun, and, in a very spook-like manner, gave us the following instructions.

"Replace this with the one he is using at the moment. Do not remove the cap. Just bend, or twist it, so that it looks as close as possible to the one you are replacing."

Inside the box was a half-used tube of Colgate toothpaste.

The following morning, with Verger well out of the way, we took a picture of the tube of Colgate he had used earlier. We swapped the tubes over and, by referring to the picture, we made sure that the new tube was lying, in exactly the same position, and was the same shape as the old one.

Our work was done.

Jamil Riaz was on the plane to Jakarta the following day to be reunited with his family.

Nothing was heard of his whereabouts or the state of his health from that day forward.

I had no idea what was in that tube of toothpaste. It was not until some years later, in the autumn of 2006, when I learned of the death of Alexander Litvinenko, a Russian spy who had been murdered in London, that I began to hazard a guess.

The success of Drugstore led to the rapprochement of Colonel Gaddafi after he was confronted with the irrefutable evidence we had gathered. Not long afterwards, the Libyan regime gave up its nuclear ambitions, and then went on to dismantle the country's Atomic Research facilities.

By then Richard's health was deteriorating rapidly. After vacating the offices in Dubai and winding up the company, Service Air, he and I were guests-of-honour at a dinner held at Fort Monkton in Gosport. We were presented with mementoes of 'Operation Drugstore' and we each received a handsome cash bonus for our efforts.

Sadly, Richard's illness had, by then, been confirmed as terminal cancer. Soon after receiving the accolades from his friends and peers, and shortly before he was to be awarded the honour of Officer of the British Empire, for his services to the government, he died in the Queen Elizabeth Hospital Portsmouth.

CHAPTER FIFTY-FIVE
WEAPONS OF MASS DESTRUCTION

By the start of the new millennium, I was a relatively experienced MI6 agent. Twenty-five years in the army had provided a good foundation for me to operate, confidently, anywhere in the world, often completely on my own and with no backup whatsoever from the office in London.

I wouldn't say that I was any braver than the next man but, I had managed to become somewhat inured to fear, and could remain calm and unperturbed in scary and, sometimes life- threatening situations. I have always found a sense of humour to be an invaluable asset.

A couple of years earlier in a bar, in a far from salubrious area of Montego Bay, I found myself surrounded by a bunch of heavy drinking cocaine dealers.

I was rather caught off-guard when the Rasta looking guy standing next to me spouted threateningly to his friends who were gathered around, "Don't speak to this guy. He works for MI5!"

Adopting my *almost too pissed to stand up* look, I faced my accuser.

"I don't know the first thing about furniture," I slurred. "And I have never, in my life, worked for MFI!"

A ripple of laughter went around the bar and the remainder of the evening was spent drinking and joking with my newly formed circle of buddies.

The most important element of being a good Secret Agent is, having the ability to convince people that you are anything but a spy working for Her Majesty's Secret Intelligence Service. I have no doubt whatsoever that I was, at some time, touched with the *Blarney Stone*, and lying was something that always came very easily to me.

I had been trained to be infiltrated and exfiltrated into, and out of, hostile territories by helicopter, boat, parachute or submarine. Most of the time, however, entry and exit were made by public transport or by simply hiring a car and driving across international borders.

Not all the operations I was involved in were carried out alone or as a couple. Quite often I would be deployed as part of a team. And not all the

197

jobs were, in any way glamorous or could even be described as interesting. One such operation involved providing a safe environment for a meeting between a senior British SIS Officer and an Iraqi agent in a hotel room in Tunis. This routine meeting resulted in, what we thought at the time, was a rather disappointing and boring outcome. It was some time later that the ramifications of that meeting were to prove far from disappointing and boring. The information gleaned from the Iraqi agent would help to shatter the illusion created by the foremost leaders of the Western World.

CHAPTER FIFTY-SIX

Just a few months prior to that meeting I had been summoned to the flat in London, and asked to consider the viability of inserting and extracting four-man patrols, clandestinely, onto target areas inside Iraq. The exact details of the targets were not given to me at that time, but I was instructed to work on the likelihood of there being as many as twenty, spread anywhere across the country.

The Russian designed and built Mi8 helicopter was one of the most successful helicopters in the world. Thousands had been manufactured in the old Soviet Union, and were not only used extensively throughout the Warsaw Pact countries but proved to be very popular with civilian operators. They had also been bought by no less than fifty countries around the globe and, most importantly to me, extensively used throughout Iraq.

I decided that I had to know more about the ubiquitous, and very well respected Mi8 – better known in military circles as the 'Hip'. While I was finding out more about it, I thought it might be a good idea if I could also make myself more useful to the government by getting myself qualified to fly it.

I spotted an advertisement in *Flight International* magazine, a publication popular with professional pilots. 'FOR SALE – Newly refurbished MI 8 and MI 17 helicopters'.

The Mi17 was an updated version of the Mi8, the engines and transmission had been upgraded to improve it's 'hot and high' capability. Both versions of the aircraft looked almost identical, the main difference being that the tail rotors were on different sides, the Mi8 having the tail rotor on the port side, and the Mi17 having it on the starboard side.

I contacted the dealer and introduced myself as Captain Bob Meacher. This was one of my aliases which were very robust and could, therefore, be used abroad operationally. I already had in place all the documentation I would need to support my cover story of being a commercial pilot who was working on behalf of a European aviation company who would, at that time, prefer to remain anonymous. I was then invited – at my own expense, of course, to inspect the aircraft which were on an airfield in Estonia.

After my usual 'dry cleaning' routine, I took the appropriate tray from Sir David Stirling's old desk and set off to the airport in my new persona, Captain Robert Meacher. I bought a business-class return ticket to Tallinn via Stockholm from the Scandinavian Airlines desk at Heathrow Airport. I paid by credit card from an account which was regularly used – paying by cash was a sure way of bringing your name to the attention of the authorities, so it was strictly taboo. I carried with me all the documentation necessary to give credibility to my newly adopted alter-ego; passport – well used and with a selection of innocuous looking entry stamps; driving and pilot licences; credit and debit cards; and an assortment of business cards, brochures and letters.

Being Bob Meacher I wore an ostentatious watch and a ring – something that Red Riley would never do. I found them to be annoying, and, of course, that is just what I wanted them to be. I wore them to help prevent Bob Meacher from perhaps signing the wrong signature or giving away wrong personal details in a moment of stress, or when too relaxed, and lacking concentration.

Whenever I travelled I would always keep a book, or a copy of the *Telegraph* crossword close to hand, to give myself an excuse to avoid getting engaged in any unwelcome cross-examination. Feigning sleep was always a good way to steer clear of any unsolicited overtures from fellow passengers on flights or train journeys.

On arrival at the Lennart Meri Airport in Tallinn, I was met by a middle-aged man in a grey suit and black tie, looking like he was either on his way to or had just come from, a funeral. In one hand, he was holding a small placard will the name 'Captain Meacher' in bold letters across it. The other hand he held up to his face while he took a long drag on his cigarette.

As I approached with my right hand extended, he quickly threw down the cigarette onto the airport floor, crushed it underfoot, and exhaled a huge plume of smoke, greeting me to Estonia with a lung full of foul-smelling nicotine.

"That's me," I said looking at the placard and emitting an affected cough.

"Welcome to Tallinn, my name is Alexi. Please, come with me and I will drive you to your hotel."

After a short while, we arrived at the Park Inn in the centre of the ancient, and somewhat grubby looking, capital city.

The following morning Alexi took me to an old, disused 'Soviet Chemistry Airfield', about an hour's drive from the city. There was a selection of Mi8 and Mi17 helicopters lined up outside the dilapidated aircraft hangars. I spent a little time looking at them, pretending to show the keen interest of a potential purchaser – then I told Alexi what I wanted.

"They look very good, and I am certainly interested in purchasing one, and quite possibly two," I said.

"But first I would like to learn how to fly this type. Can you please introduce me to someone who might be able to do that?"

His eyes lit up at the prospect of a potential sale.

"Please give me a moment," he said, reaching for his mobile phone.

I continued to play the game, of looking interested, and continued with my inspection for the next half an hour, while Alexi made a few calls.

Putting his phone into his pocket as he walked towards me with a smile on his face, he said.

"I have a very good friend who is a major in the National Reserve Air Force who is able to teach you. But first, you must pay ten thousand US dollars for ten hours flying training."

"When can we start?" I asked, jumping down from the open tailgate.

His hand went back into his pocket. Another lengthy phone call, and then he said, "So long as you have paid me the money, then you will be able to start tomorrow."

There was always a reasonable amount of money left in each of my alias accounts to be used as a float or to be available for a quick deployment if one should become necessary, so getting hold of the ten thousand dollars did not prove to be hugely difficult.

The following evening, I rang Alexi and told him that I had the money and I was ready to get started.

The introduction to my new flying instructor took me a little by surprise.

"This is my good friend Marion," said Alexi, as we walked towards the waiting helicopter.

My instructor was indeed, a major in the National Guard, the military-style flying suit leaving me in do doubt whatsoever. Apart from the badges of rank displayed on each shoulder, there were also numerous formation badges and medal ribbons. I later learned that the medals had been awarded for service in Afghanistan, where a long and bloody war had been fought in the nineteen eighties when Estonia was still a part of the Soviet Union.

Marion the Major spoke good English and, picking the words carefully, in a very soft voice spoke to me, as if telling me a story.

"When I was born in 1953, my mother and father very much liked the American movie star John Wayne. You may not know, but John Wayne had the real name, Marion. And that is why they named me, their first-born son, after their hero.

The flying training was fun. Marion was a good instructor, and the Mi8 was very easy to fly.

The most difficult thing to get used to was reading the gauges and instruments in the cockpit, which were all written in Russian Cyrillic. The altitude was indicated in metres, and the airspeed in kilometres per hour, rather than feet and knots, which were the units used in, just about, every other part of the world.

After the ten hours of flying were completed my instructor and I both agreed that I was more than competent to fly and operate the aircraft unsupervised.

After pocketing the improvised Certificate of Qualification to act as captain, I slipped a bottle of Jack Daniels finest 'firewater' into the old cowboy's saddlebag, as a thank you present, and watched him ride off into the sunset.

Before I left I told Alexi that I was very interested in doing a deal with him, and would contact him as soon as I got back home. I never did, of course.

CHAPTER FIFTY-SEVEN

Back in London, I explained that, in order to reach targets anywhere in Iraq, I would need to have available to me an Mi8 or 17, painted in Iraqi military livery, adapted for Night Vision Goggles, and fitted with auxiliary fuel tanks. The extra fuel capacity would give us a useful range of about one thousand nautical miles. With twelve troops on board, I would have to launch, at night, either from Kuwait or Jordan. My controller accepted, in principle, that the undertaking was viable, and it was then allocated the code-name Operation Larkspur.

With the method of inserting the four-man patrols then, more-or-less, organised, I next needed to liaise with the guys who I would be dropping off. And that would mean a visit to my old stomping ground of Sterling Lines, Hereford, home of the SAS.

The sergeant major of the 'increment' at that time, otherwise known as Revolutionary Warfare Wing (RWW), was Carl Ryder. Carl was someone who I had lived almost next door to for many years, and we had watched each other's children growing up together.

I briefed him on the progress of Larkspur, to date, and he was happy, in principle, with our proposed method of insertion and extraction. RWW would provide a team of twelve, armed with as many laser target designators (LTDs) as they could lay their hands on, and mark the targets inside Iraq, once the details of the locations were passed to us.

The LTD was a lightweight, portable device which, when activated, would direct a pulse of laser beams onto a target. The reflected beams could then be identified by a laser-guided munition, such as the Paveway five-hundred-pound, laser-guided bomb.

In order for the teams to position the LTDs covertly, they would need to be dropped off, at least three kilometres, away from each target. They would then walk until they could positively identify the target, and set up the device. Once in position, the LTD could then be left, and activated, remotely, at a later date. Unless, of course, the apparatus was stumbled upon by some innocent goatherd or the like. To minimise the risk of that happening, the team would need to spend time camouflaging the designators and, if considered to be necessary, laying booby-traps. The booby-traps, when triggered by a trip-wire, would destroy the equipment by strategically placed explosives.

Bearing in mind all the relevant factors, we decided to allow four hours on the ground for each target to be marked efficiently. We would, therefore, recommend that three four-man patrols would be inserted, under the cover of darkness, to mark one target each. If we were provided with the details of twenty targets, as was earlier suggested, then we would need seven nights to complete the operation.

The officer-in-command of the increment, Major Keith Eglington, and Carl, were at the next operational planning meeting in London. The plan was accepted and would be activated once the necessary ministerial approval had been granted, and details of the weapons of mass destruction (WMDs) sites, had been confirmed by an agent from inside Iraq.

At the meeting in Tunisia, which had taken place only a few months before the invasion of Iraq, the agent confirmed, quite unequivocally, that any WMDs, including stockpiles of gas, had already been dismantled or destroyed.

Shortly after our operational meeting in London, Operation Larkspur was cancelled.

CHAPTER FIFTY-EIGHT
25th DECEMBER 2004 1528 HOURS

I was tucking into Christmas dinner when the phone rang.

It was my daughter Nina, who was on her honeymoon in Thailand, moaning about having an earache.

"What's the best thing to do for it, Dad?" she pleaded to me pitifully.

I had knocked back champagne before dinner and one or two large glasses of red wine during it. Not having the faintest idea of what to do about an earache I put the question to the guests around the table.

"Anyone got a guaranteed cure for an earache?" I shouted to the twelve friends and family.

A number of recommendations were offered up from the diners who were also, by then, pretty well on their way with the wine.

"Cotton wool soaked in warm olive oil and rammed into the lug-hole. Never been known to fail," offered our friend Karen.

"My dear departed grandmother used to drown a cockroach in whisky. Stick the insect into her ear and drink the whisky. If it failed to have an immediate effect she would administer further doses, but without the cockroach, until the bottle was empty," slurred Karon's husband Tim, who was as high as a kite even before dinner had started.

"No, no, no," said Kathy seriously. "Hot raisins are what she needs. If she can't get hold of raisins, then she should try the heart of an onion."

Pain in the arse brother-in-law Graham, was next to add his pearl of wisdom.

"It's her honeymoon, for Christ's sake," he shouted, spraying bits of, half-eaten, turkey across the table. "She should have better things to do with her time than worry about an earache."

"Well, there you are Nina," I said. "A few ideas for you to consider, but probably best if you just have a lie-down. It must be getting quite late with you. Give me a call in the morning. No, on second thoughts, make that the afternoon, and let us know how you are. Goodnight love."

I was in bed in a deep, alcohol-induced, sleep when the phone screamed next to my ear.

"Who the fuck can that be at this time of the morning?" I chuntered to myself, fumbling to pick up the phone.

It was Nina again. "Dad! I don't know what to do."

I interrupted her. "Honestly Ni, I'm sorry, but there is nothing I can do for your earache."

"It's not that Dad," she said. "We went down to the beach for breakfast this morning and the sea has disappeared!"

"Don't be ridiculous Nina. The sea can't just disappear," I said softly. Well aware that she did have a tendency to exaggerate somewhat.

"Honestly Dad, it has. People in the hotel are telling us that a tsunami is on the way and that we should run to the hills."

"A tsunami! What the fuck is a tsunami?" I said as the phone line went dead.

"Really. My daughter and her vivid imagination," I thought to myself as I settled back down to sleep.

The next morning there was nothing on the BBC news other than the enormous earthquake that had struck, just after midnight, in the Indian Ocean, and the ensuing tsunami which had hit most of the bordering land-mass including, of course, Thailand.

The mountain wave or tsunami had risen to a height of over one hundred feet and travelled across the ocean at the staggering speed of more than five hundred miles an hour.

Most of the Western coastal area of Thailand had been engulfed and there were reports of as many as a quarter of a million people being killed.

I felt sick with worry and desperately tried to get in touch with Nina's hotel, but found it to be impossible to get through. The thought of losing my daughter was far worse than any emotions that I had felt at any time during my military career, or my time as an MI6 agent.

Television reports showed dramatic pictures of the hotel where Nina, and her new husband Tom, had been booked into but had been upgraded for their honeymoon. The hotel was completely destroyed and there were thought to be no survivors.

It wasn't until the day after Boxing Day that I received a call from Tom, telling me that both he and Nina were safe and unharmed. Nina was how-ever very shocked and distressed. She then came on the line and begged me to hire a plane and fly out to get them both home.

Nina always did think of me as some sort of wonderful SAS hero, who was capable of doing, just about, anything. I wasn't, of course. And given the circumstances all across the affected area, it would have been almost impossible for anyone to hire a private jet and fly out to get them home, even for her 'super dad'.

The newlyweds got back safely a few days after the traumatic events and Nina seemed to settle down well. It wasn't until some months later that the shock of the Indian Ocean tsunami would start to have a devastating impact on my beautiful and vivacious daughter's health.

One of the many skills I was required to maintain proficiency in as an agent, was skiing. At least once a year, the service would arrange, and pay for, a skiing trip for a couple of weeks, normally in Norway.

But this jaunt was at my expense, and not in Norway but in Chamonix in the French Alps. Nina and I had just raced each other down a Red Run and were in a small queue of people waiting for the chair-lift. As we stood casually chatting Nina took a small step forward and unexpectedly fell to the ground.

"What the hell is up with you?" I asked with a laugh. "People tend to fall while they are coming down the piste. Not while they are standing in the bloody queue."

"I'm scared Dad," she said. "There's something wrong with my legs."

We didn't know it at the time, but that fall was the first indication that Nina had contracted the debilitating condition multiple sclerosis, known as MS, which she was convinced was brought on by the horrific events in Thailand the previous Christmas.

Back in London, we went together to the Chelsea and Westminster Hospital where, after a series of tests, Nina was diagnosed with Primary Progressive MS.

Over the following few months, we tried everything we could to alleviate the inexorable advance of the disease. We diligently searched the internet to find some sort of cure, convinced that there must have been a newly developed remedy somewhere in the world. We were willing to try anything. We tried barometric chamber treatment; Chinese tablets that cost an absolute fortune; a trip to a hospital in Hungary, where it was claimed that an insert into an artery leading to the brain was the very latest breakthrough and was providing wonderful results. None of them worked for Nina.

After a while, we were convinced that we had found the solution. We identified a 'world-renowned' expert in MS who had his offices in Harley Street, London. For only two thousand pounds per visit, the consultant would examine Nina and give her some drugs to take. The drugs proved to be totally useless and the so-called 'world-renowned expert' turned out to be nothing more than a fake who had rented a room in a Harley Street clinic on an hourly basis, just for our visits.

We came to realise that our efforts were futile. There was nothing that could stop the relentless progress of multiple sclerosis.

Now, my once vibrant and ebullient daughter, though still beautiful and full of fun, cannot work and is confined to a wheelchair. Her sight is rapidly deteriorating and she has very little strength in her arms.

Watching her waste away has been the most harrowing and painful experience of my life.

CHAPTER FIFTY-NINE
RADCLIFFE ENGLAND
11th NOVEMBER 2015 0552 HOURS

"Sweet mother of Jesus," I say to myself. Remembering the words my long-deceased father used to say, the nearest thing he ever got to blaspheming. The strongest swear word I ever recall him using apart from 'Blast' was 'Bloody'.

It's a little after five in the morning and I'm struggling to understand why I have dragged myself out of bed so early. It's fucking freezing! I can even see my breath. I wriggle my toes in the vain hope of returning some circulation to my bare, but pristine as ever, feet. I suppose I should expect it to be cold, it is, after all, the middle of winter in the small suburb of Radcliffe, North Manchester. Whilst waiting for the kettle to boil I chuckle to myself, confirming how ridiculous I must look, as I catch a glimpse of my reflection in the glass door, wearing nothing but my partner Carol's fluffy pink dressing gown.

I clear away the icy condensation from the window and look out towards the bottom of the garden. Even though it is not due to get light for, at least, another two hours, I can clearly make out the sun. The sun I refer to is the *Sun* newspaper which is plastered across our neighbour's bedroom window. The yellow glow of the streetlight illuminating the headline of September 11th 2001: 'DAY THAT CHANGED THE WORLD'. I find it hard to comprehend why anyone would use old newspapers as curtains. But then again Radcliffe is not noted for being the most salubrious of neighbourhoods.

As I stand in front of the glass door stirring my tea, I once again, consider the image in front of me. Still a fine figure of a man, I manage to convince myself, even though I am now knocking on seventy. I have an appointment at eight in the Doctor's Surgery, on the first floor of the Business Jet Centre in Manchester Airport. The appointment is for my annual assessment, which I must pass to maintain my flying licence. Doctor Reisler, who has been doing my medicals for the past twenty years or so, knows that I am deaf in my left ear due to all the shooting I did as a young man in the Army. He also knows that I have worked out how to cheat when taking the Audio

Gram test. He gives me a knowing look and smiles as he signs the certificate indicating that I am fit to fly. Before handing me the form he reminds me to always carry my reading glasses in the cockpit whilst flying, in order for me to be able to read the instruments clearly. I return the smile and promise I will as always – but I never do, and I think the good doctor knows that.

The sound of our cat, Ginge, scratching to get in after his night on the tiles, and the kids shouting next door, as they awaken, brings me back to reality. I have no idea how long I have been stirring my brew for but it looks more like treacle than it does tea.

The sound of a car and headlights suddenly flooding the kitchen as it pulls up outside the door seems to be very unusual for this time of the morning in our quiet little cul-de-sac.

How weird… I think, as one door slams, quickly followed by another.

Footsteps… Two people… one male, one female I guess.

Stranger still is the urgent banging on the front door. It's aggressively persistent and probably much louder than necessary given the ridiculously early hour.

As I open the door, for some obscure reason, I am almost expecting what greets me.

"Mister Patrick James Riley?" the man in a suit and tie asks.

I nod, but only to acknowledge that that is who I am. I am more concerned with wrapping the, rather fetching, pink dressing gown clumsily around my body to conserve, what little bit of dignity I am managing to hold on to intact.

The man in the suit introduces himself.

"I am Detective Inspector Polenski, and this is Detective Constable Julie Green from Lancashire police." He glances at his young colleague and then back at me. "I am arresting you for the murder of Howard Paul Riley on or about the twentieth of January 1990."

He then proceeds to caution me and explains to me my rights, before producing a set of handcuffs.

"Ok," I say. "So, what happens next?"

Lightning Source UK Ltd.
Milton Keynes UK
UKHW041630280519

R1905400001B/R19054PG343267UKX1B/1/P